MILLER JAMES HUGGINS

DAVID MARK WINFIELD

W9-AXP-670

JOHN FRANKLIN BAKER

OSBORNE EARL SMITH
"Ozzie" "The Wizard"

KIRBY PUCKETT

ROBIN R. YOUNT

JOSEPH WILLIAMS

JOSEPH WILLIAMS

DONALD HOWARD SUTTON

FRANK GIBSON SELEE

LYNN NOLAN RYAN JR

GEORGE HERMAN (BABE) RUTH

GEORGE LEE ANDERSON

JACOB NELSON FOX
"NELLIE"

# HALL OF FAME PLAYERS
# COOPERSTOWN

Bruce Herman

Publications International, Ltd.

Bruce Herman is a sportswriter and editor who has served as editorial consultant for the Topps Company since 1991. A contributing writer for the books *100 Years of Baseball* and *The Golden Age of Baseball,* Herman has contributed to *Sports Illustrated* and many other major publications. He also has been internationally syndicated by Tribune Media. He writes regularly for Major League Baseball Publications and Athlon Sports.

Copyright © 2008 Publications International, Ltd. All rights reserved.
This book may not be reproduced or quoted in whole or in part by any means whatsoever without written permission from:

Louis Weber, CEO
Publications International, Ltd.
7373 North Cicero Avenue
Lincolnwood, Illinois 60712

Permission is never granted for commercial purposes.

ISBN-13: 978-1-4127-1383-2
ISBN-10: 1-4127-1383-8

Manufactured in China.

8 7 6 5 4 3 2 1

Library of Congress Control Number: 2006939554

# CONTENTS

# Welcome to
# Baseball's Hall of Fame

Everyone knows that Abner Doubleday invented baseball in 1839, right? Or perhaps Alexander Cartwright and his Knickerbockers club invented it in 1845. Or maybe it sprouted and evolved from various children's games played as early as the 18th century. But in 1907, a panel of "experts" declared that the game was the brainchild of Doubleday, fashioned in the

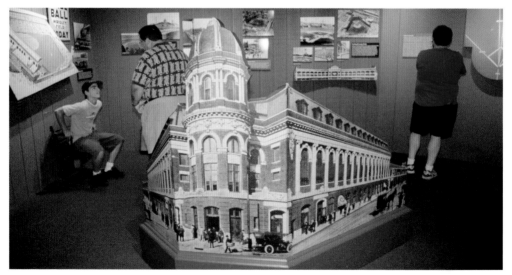

*Classic Ballparks Exhibit (top) and plaques wall room (right)*

*Memorabilia at the Baseball Hall of Fame*

tiny New York town of Cooperstown, where the future Civil War hero coined the word, designed the diamond, and crafted the rules. (Truth be told, most historians now conclude that all of this would be news to Doubleday.)

No matter, the game took on a life of its own and robustly rooted itself into the American culture. In 1939, 100 years after Doubleday supposedly laid the foundation, a shrine was built to honor the sport's greatest heroes. On June 12, 1939, 25 stars and legends of the game (elected over the previous three years) were inducted with ornate spectacle into the National Baseball

Hall of Fame located in—of course—Cooperstown, where the 15,000 spectators that lined Main Street represented many times over the actual population of the town.

The requirement for inclusion is rigorous: A person needs to obtain at least 75 percent of the vote from either the Baseball Writers Association of America or a special veterans' committee. The formula, essentially unchanged to this day, has yielded an average of less than four inductees per year through 2007. What began as a one-room, 1,200-square-foot museum built at a cost of $100,000 is now home to nearly three million artifacts and library items. Attendance has soared from about 25,000 visitors in 1939 to more than 350,000 annually.

## Red-Letter Dates

**1936** Hall of Fame is established and first inductions are made

**1939** Museum is opened in Cooperstown

**1950** Major new wing is added

**1958** Plaque gallery debuts

**1962** Jackie Robinson is the first African American elected

**1968** National Baseball Library is established

**1973** Roberto Clemente is first Latino player elected

**1994** Major Library expansion; research facility is added

**2001** Museum welcomes its 12,000,000th visitor

**2004** Major two-year renovation is completed

# 1936: The First Class

**CHRISTY MATHEWSON**
NEW YORK, N.L. 1900–1916
CINCINNATI, N.L. 1916
BORN FACTORYVILLE, PA. AUGUST 12, 1880
GREATEST OF ALL THE GREAT PITCHERS
IN THE 20TH CENTURY'S FIRST QUARTER
PITCHED 3 SHUTOUTS IN 1905 WORLD SERIES.
FIRST PITCHER OF THE GREAT EVER TO
WIN 30 GAMES IN 3 SUCCESSIVE YEARS.
WON 37 GAMES IN 1908
"MATTY WAS MASTER OF THEM ALL"

**HONUS WAGNER**
LOUISVILLE, N.L. 1897–1899
PITTSBURGH, N.L. 1900–1917
THE GREATEST SHORTSTOP IN BASEBALL
HISTORY. BORN CARNEGIE, PA., FEB. 24, 1874
KNOWN TO FANS AS "HONUS," "HANS" AND
"THE FLYING DUTCHMAN", RETIRED IN 1917,
HAVING SCORED MORE RUNS, MADE MORE
HITS AND STOLEN MORE BASES THAN
ANY OTHER PLAYER IN THE HISTORY
OF HIS LEAGUE

**TYRUS RAYMOND COBB**
DETROIT–PHILADELPHIA, A.L. 1905–1928
LED AMERICAN LEAGUE IN BATTING
TWELVE TIMES AND CREATED OR
EQUALLED MORE MAJOR LEAGUE
RECORDS THAN ANY OTHER PLAYER.
RETIRED WITH .410 MAJOR LEAGUE HITS.

**GEORGE HERMAN (BABE) RUTH**
BOSTON–NEW YORK, A.L. BOSTON, N.L.
1915–1935
GREATEST DRAWING CARD IN HISTORY OF
BASEBALL, HOLDER OF MANY HOME RUN
AND OTHER BATTING RECORDS, GATHERED
714 HOME RUNS IN ADDITION TO FIFTEEN
IN WORLD SERIES.

**WALTER PERRY JOHNSON**
WASHINGTON 1907–1927
CONCEDED TO BE FASTEST BALL PITCHER
IN HISTORY OF GAME. WON 414 GAMES
WITH LOSING TEAM BEHIND HIM MANY YEARS
HOLDER OF STRIKE OUT AND SHUT OUT RECORDS

> "It's everybody's game, everybody's party.
> Play ball, America!"

---

—Kenesaw Mountain Landis, introductory message in the
Official Program of the Hall of Fame Opening in 1939

## The Class of 1936

The first year of elections yielded this inaugural group of greats.

Ty Cobb: "Most elusive of batters, as well as most effective…was as clever with the short hit as with the long drive."

Walter Johnson: "Of fabulous pitching speed."

Christy Mathewson: "The skill of his great arm, and that courage that was his is lost, but his memory is green in the heart of every enthusiast."

Babe Ruth: "Possessor of stout arms, the stout heart and the sharp eye that picked only the best ones, but when he did pick one, oh how he hit it!"

Honus Wagner: "Who never has been equaled as a batter and fielder, not even by his mates in the Hall of Fame."

"If you don't feel an aura that's almost spiritual when you walk through the Hall of Fame, then check tomorrow's obituary: You're in it."

---

—Don Sutton

An American League ("The Collins") vs. National League ("The Wagners") all-star game was played on the day the Hall of Fame opened in 1939. Eleven of the players who participated would one day be inducted.

"A lot of people question old times. They question what has gone before. They question past generations. And that's their privilege. But without the memories of the past, there could be no dreams of greatness in the future; without those passing yesterdays, there could be no bright tomorrows."

---

—Ford Frick

# Centennial Stats

Baseball was officially declared to be 100 years old when the Hall of Fame was dedicated in 1939. Listed are the career statistical leaders of the game's first century.

| BATTING | | |
|---|---|---|
| Average | Ty Cobb | .366 |
| Doubles | Tris Speaker | 792 |
| Triples | Sam Crawford | 309 |
| Home Runs | Babe Ruth | 714 |
| RBI | Babe Ruth | 2,210 |
| Hits | Ty Cobb | 4,189 |
| Extra-base Hits | Babe Ruth | 1,356 |
| Total Bases | Ty Cobb | 5,857 |
| Runs | Ty Cobb | 2,245 |
| Walks | Babe Ruth | 2,062 |
| Stolen Bases | Billy Hamilton | 912 |
| PITCHING | | |
| Wins | Cy Young | 511 |
| ERA | Ed Walsh | 1.82 |
| Winning Pct. | Bob Caruthers | 218–99, .688 |
| Games | Cy Young | 906 |
| Complete Games | Cy Young | 749 |
| Shutouts | Walter Johnson | 110 |
| Strikeouts | Walter Johnson | 3,509 |

(Based on a minimum of 2,000 plate appearances or 2,000 innings pitched through 1938.)

# CHAPTER ONE
## ON THE CORNERS

## "May it forever stand as a symbol of clean play and good sportsmanship."

—Kenesaw Mountain Landis, officially declaring the Hall of Fame open in 1939

First Hall of Fame class (1939): Front Row (left to right): Eddie Collins, Babe Ruth, Connie Mack, Cy Young; Back Row: Honus Wagner, Grover Cleveland Alexander, Tris Speaker, Napoleon Lajoie, George Sisler, Walter Johnson

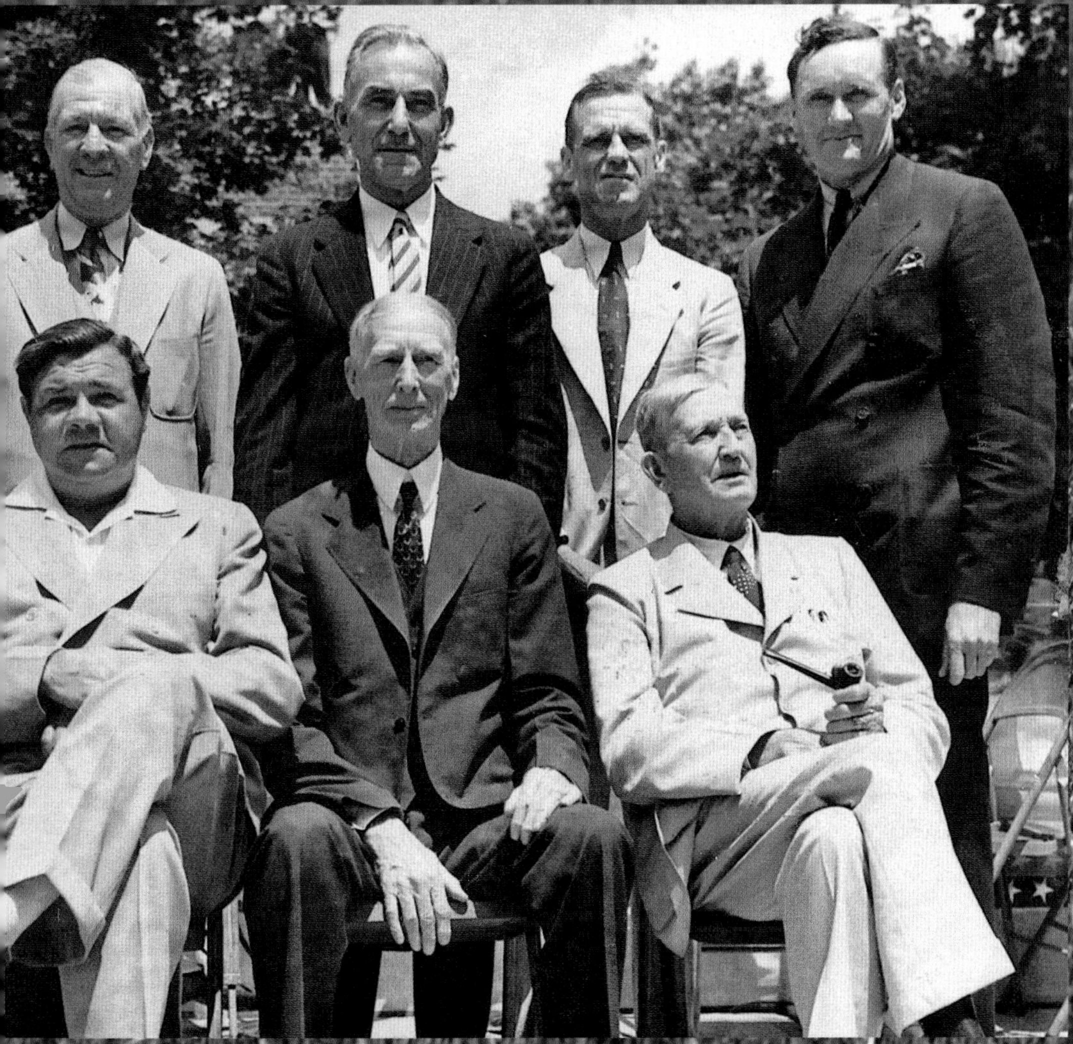

# WILLIE McCOVEY

## FIRST BASEMAN ◊ ELECTED 1986

If ever a player walked softly and carried a big stick, it was Willie McCovey. Brandishing a 38-ounce bat, the soft-spoken, towering first baseman hammered more home runs (521) than any left-handed batter in National League history save Barry Bonds. Playing 19 of his 22 seasons for the Giants, the 1969 NL MVP set a senior circuit career record with 18 grand slams.

"I'd walk me."

—McCovey, on how he would pitch to himself

# JIMMIE FOXX

## FIRST BASEMAN ❧ ELECTED 1951

Jimmie Foxx once described his batting style by saying, "I wanted to leave my fingerprints on the wood." He left his fingerprints on the game by smashing 534 home runs (second to Babe Ruth's 714 until 1966) and capturing three AL MVP Awards. One of those was for the Philadelphia Athletics in 1933, when "The Beast" batted .356, knocked home 163 runs, and hit 48 home runs to win the Triple Crown.

"Next to Joe DiMaggio, Foxx was the greatest player I ever saw. When Foxx hit a ball, it sounded like gunfire."

—Ted Williams

# GEORGE BRETT

**THIRD BASEMAN / FIRST BASEMAN ⚾ ELECTED 1999**

• In 1980, Brett flirted with a .400 batting average for much of the season. He was sitting on the "magic number" on September 19 before finishing the season at .390. He still won the second of his three batting crowns and an MVP Award.

• In Kansas City's 1985 championship season, Brett was the ALCS MVP and a .370 hitter in the World Series.

• He remains the only player in major-league history to amass 3,000 hits, 300 homers, 600 doubles, 100 triples, 1,500 RBI, and 200 steals.

# STICKY SITUATION

On July 24, 1983, George Brett blasted a ninth-inning, two-run homer that put his Kansas City Royals ahead of the Yankees, 5–4. Umpire Tim McClelland, however, called him out for slathering pine tar too high up the bat, and— following Brett's apoplectic rage— New York held on for an apparent win. After four days of deliberation by the league, the ruling was reversed, the game was replayed from that point, and Kansas City won. Brett owns the bat, but he has loaned it to the Hall for its "Baseball As America" traveling exhibition.

# TAKING INVENTORY

## FIRST-BALLOT HALL OF FAMERS

| PLAYER | POSITION(S) | YEAR ELECTED |
|---|---|---|
| Hank Aaron | outfield | 1982 |
| Ernie Banks | shortstop/first base | 1977 |
| Johnny Bench | catcher | 1989 |
| Wade Boggs | third base | 2005 |
| George Brett | third base | 1999 |
| Lou Brock | outfield | 1985 |
| Rod Carew | second base/first base | 1991 |
| Steve Carlton | pitcher | 1994 |
| Dennis Eckersley | pitcher | 2004 |
| Bob Feller | pitcher | 1962 |
| Bob Gibson | pitcher | 1981 |
| Tony Gwynn | outfield | 2007 |
| Reggie Jackson | outfield | 1993 |
| Al Kaline | outfield | 1980 |
| Sandy Koufax | pitcher | 1972 |
| Mickey Mantle | outfield/first base | 1974 |
| Willie Mays | outfield | 1979 |

# HARMON KILLEBREW

**FIRST BASEMAN / THIRD BASEMAN / OUTFIELDER  ELECTED 1984**

"He hit line drives that put the opposition in jeopardy. And I don't mean infielders, I mean outfielders."

—Ossie Bluege, the scout who signed Killebrew

Harmon Killebrew was the embodiment of the phrase "farmboy power." The son of an Idaho sheriff/professional wrestler (whose own grandfather was said to be the strongest Union soldier in the Civil War), "Killer" was a monstrous, mild-mannered masher. He muscled 573 home runs, won the 1969 AL MVP Award for the Twins, and was the first player ever to make the All-Star team at three positions (1B, 3B, and OF).

# NEW YORK YANKEES

**If you were the Yankees manager, wouldn't you like to present this lineup card to the umpire?**

| | | |
|---|---|---|
| Catcher | Yogi Berra | 1946–1963 |
| First Base | Lou Gehrig | 1923–1939 |
| Second Base | Tony Lazzeri | 1926–1937 |
| Third Base | Wade Boggs | 1993–1997 |
| Shortstop | Phil Rizzuto | 1941–1942, 1946–1956 |
| Outfield | Babe Ruth | 1920–1934 |
| Outfield | Joe DiMaggio | 1936–1942, 1946–1951 |
| Outfield | Mickey Mantle | 1951–1968 |
| Pitcher | Whitey Ford | 1950, 1953–1967 |

# LOU GEHRIG

## FIRST BASEMAN ⚾ ELECTED 1939

From humble beginnings strode "The Iron Horse." Ludwig Heinrich Gehrig was the son of German immigrants and the only one of four siblings to survive. When he was nine years old, his father gave him a catcher's mitt for the wrong hand. At 14, he hit .170 for his high school team. Yet three generations after his death at age 37, Gehrig remains one of the most beloved figures in sports history.

Between 1926 and 1932, he and Babe Ruth formed the nucleus of an order that powered the Yankees to four World Series wins. Gehrig was a formidable force even without "The Babe"; he lead the Yanks to consecutive world championships in 1936, 1937, and 1938. Gehrig, who earned his nickname by playing in 2,130 consecutive games, won two MVP Awards and the 1934 Triple Crown. His parlay of 493 home runs, 1,995 RBI, 1,509 walks, and a .340 average has been equaled only by The Babe himself.

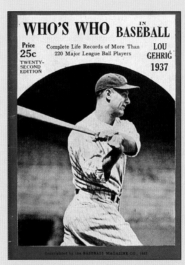

WHO'S WHO IN BASEBALL
Price 25c
TWENTY-SECOND EDITION
Complete Life Records of More Than 220 Major League Ball Players
LOU GEHRIG 1937

Copyrighted by the BASEBALL MAGAZINE CO., 1937

"Gehrig never learned that a ballplayer couldn't be good every day."

—Hank Gowdy

# THE CURSE OF THE IRON HORSE

As if it wasn't bad enough that the Red Sox made the bonehead deal of all time by selling Babe Ruth to the Yankees in 1920, consider this: Five years later, the Bronx Bombers offered a 21-year-old named Lou Gehrig to Boston for a first baseman named Phil Todt. The Sox turned them down.

# DAN BROUTHERS

**FIRST BASEMAN ⚊ ELECTED 1945**

"I don't think I ever saw a longer hitter," said immortal manager John McGraw of "Big Dan"—a rare 200-pounder in 19th-century ball. Brouthers, a barehanded first baseman who played for 11 teams, won more batting titles (five) prior to 1900 than anyone else, and only three players of that era hit more than his 106 home runs.

# EDDIE MURRAY

**FIRST BASEMAN**  **ELECTED 2003**

## Greatest Switch-hitter Ever?

**All-Time Switch-Hit Rankings ......**

RBI.................................................................

Extra-Base Hits...............................................

Intentional Walks.............................................

HRs/Each Side, Same Game..............................

Hits.................................................................

Home Runs.......................................................

Total Bases......................................................

Doubles............................................................

Runs Scored.....................................................

| ...Murray | ..........Leader |
| --- | --- |
| ....1st (1,917) | ..........Murray |
| ....1st (1,099) | ..........Murray |
| ....1st (222) | ..............Murray |
| ....1st (11) | ................Murray |
| ....2nd (3,255) | .........Pete Rose (4,256) |
| ....2nd (504) | ............Mickey Mantle (536) |
| ....2nd (5,397) | .........Pete Rose (5,752) |
| ....2nd (560) | ............Pete Rose (746) |
| ....3rd (1,627) | .........Pete Rose (2,165) |

# MAGIC NUMBERS

**3** Major-league games Ryne Sandberg saw in person before he ever played in one

**23** Hall of Fame inductees from the Giants, the most from any franchise

**59** Satchel Paige's age when he pitched his final game

**19** Of the top 20 triples hitters in history, 19 are Hall of Famers

**115** Consecutive games without striking out, a record set by Joe Sewell

# "I don't think Spahn will ever get into the Hall of Fame. He'll never stop pitching."

—Stan Musial, on a 44-year-old Spahn in 1965

# COOPERSTOWN: "AMERICA'S VILLAGE"

The heart of the most distinctly American game could beat in no more appropriate place than Cooperstown, the very definition of *Americana*. Home to barely 2,000 residents, Cooperstown has a quaint village commerce, a picturesque setting in upstate New York, and, of course, the National Baseball Hall of Fame and Museum, which attracts more than 350,000 visitors annually.

**"This is just a wonderful little city, town, or village or whatever we call it. It puts me in mind of Sleepy Hollow."**

**—Honus Wagner, at the 1939 inaugural induction ceremony**

Founded by William Cooper in the late 18th century, the village's beauty inspired a string of classic novels by his son, James Fenimore Cooper.

*The facade of the National Baseball Hall of Fame and Museum*

Cooperstown rests on the shores of Lake Otsego—dubbed "Glimmerglass" by the writer, who described it as "a broad sheet of water, so placid and limpid that it resembled a bed of the pure mountain atmosphere, compressed into a setting of hills and woods."

*An aerial view of Doubleday Stadium in Cooperstown, New York*

Cooperstown has carefully preserved its charm. It is a rare fast food-free zone; there is only one traffic light in the city; and there are no generic malls. Nearly 70 years have passed since the Hall opened during an era when the town's motto was "Where Nature Smiles." Happily, it still does.

Cost of hotel room when Hall opened in **1939: $1.** Cost of hotel room for recent induction ceremonies: **$300.00 and up**

# ORLANDO CEPEDA

## FIRST BASEMAN / OUTFIELDER ✦ ELECTED 1999

Signed out of Puerto Rico in 1955 for $500, which he used to pay for his father's funeral, "The Baby Bull" had more home runs (221) by his 27th birthday than did Hank Aaron (219). A severe knee injury in 1965 crippled his pace, but Cepeda was the unanimous 1967 NL MVP for the world-champion Cardinals. He called it quits in 1974 after pasting 379 long balls and nabbing a pair of RBI crowns.

# MIKE SCHMIDT

**THIRD BASEMAN ● ELECTED 1995**

"I don't think
I can get into
my deep inner
thoughts

about
**hitting.**
It's like
talking about
**religion.**"

—Schmidt

In 1963, a 13-year-old Schmidt was in the stands when Pete Rose made his major-league debut. Nine years later, "Michael Jack" began his own career, one that many agree certifies him as the most complete third baseman of all time. He is the home run leader at the position, as well as a winner of ten Gold Gloves and three NL MVP Awards.

"When they start the game, they don't yell 'Work Ball!' They say 'Play Ball!'"

—Willie Stargell

COOPERSTOWN 36 ON THE CORNERS

# PAUL MOLITOR

**THIRD BASEMAN / SECOND BASEMAN / FIRST BASEMAN / DESIGNATED HITTER ELECTED 2004**

"There's only **one way to play...**

whether it's the World Series or spring training."

—Molitor

• **1993:** Became, at 37, the oldest player ever to record his first 100-RBI season. Voted World Series MVP for the Blue Jays, going 12-for-24 with two doubles, two triples, two homers, and eight RBI.

• **1996:** At 40, matched his career high with a .341 average, ranking among the AL's top 10 for the 11th time.

• **Career:** The only player in history with a .300 average, 200 home runs, and 500 stolen bases.

# BROOKS ROBINSON

## THIRD BASEMAN ● ELECTED 1983

Many major-leaguers are more athletic than Brooks Robinson—Olympic track champ Jesse Owens once said Robinson ran "like a duck"—but not one of them ever played third base the way he did. The Orioles great was a clutch performer who won MVP Awards in the American League (1964), All-Star Game (1966), and World Series (1970).

**All-Time Gold Gloves by Non-Pitchers**

| | |
|---|---:|
| Brooks Robinson, 3B | 16 |
| Ozzie Smith, SS | 13 |
| Roberto Clemente, OF | 12 |
| Willie Mays, OF | 12 |
| Keith Hernandez, 1B | 11 |

"When Neil Armstrong first set foot on the moon, he and all the space scientists were puzzled by an **unidentifiable white object.** That was a home run ball hit off me in 1937 by Jimmie Foxx."

—**Lefty Gomez**

# CAP ANSON

**FIRST BASEMAN / THIRD BASEMAN ▪ ELECTED 1939**

CHICAGO.

ANSON.

FIRST BASEMAN.

Upon his 1897 retirement, Cap Anson was the game's greatest player—a .300 hitter in 24 of his 27 seasons. As a five-time National League-champion manager of the Chicago White Stockings, Anson is often credited for the "invention" of everything from spring training to the hit-and-run play. Yet any biography must include his strident racism and rigorous efforts to erect a color barrier in the game.

### Adrian Constantine Anson's Nicknames

- Ada
- Ady
- Anse
- Baby
- Cap
- Hoss

- The Marshalltown Infant
- Old Man
- Pop
- The Swede
- Uncle

# BATHING IN VICTORY

In 1897, Cubs first baseman/manager Cap Anson got himself tossed from a game for arguing that it should have been called after eight innings because of darkness. He had already sent his reserves to the showers, so when play resumed, his team had only eight players. Left fielder George Decker moved to first to replace Anson, and pitcher Don Friend rushed out to cover left—in his bathrobe. Giants manager Bill Joyce protested so long about the uniform violation that it did indeed become too dark to play, and Anson had himself a 7–5 win.

# EDDIE MATHEWS

## THIRD BASEMAN ⚜ ELECTED 1978

Until Willie McCovey launched his 513th in 1979, Eddie Mathews was the most prolific left-handed home run hitter this side of Babe Ruth and Ted Williams. And until Mike Schmidt ran him down in 1986, no third baseman had ever cleared more fences. The competitive Mathews punched at least two future Hall of Famers in his career (Don Drysdale and Frank Robinson) and pummeled two others with milestone home runs (No. 300 off Robin Roberts and No. 500 off Juan Marichal).

"I've only known three or four perfect swings in my time. This lad has one of them."

—Ty Cobb

# TONY PEREZ

**FIRST BASEMAN / THIRD BASEMAN ● ELECTED 2000**

The only stat in which Tony Perez ever led the league was double plays grounded into, but for sheer, consistent production and winning leadership, there have been few like him. He simply drove in runs: 1,652 of them (10th-most ever by a right-handed hitter), including 200 for Cincinnati's 1975 and '76 "Big Red Machine" world champs.

**"If the game lasts long enough, Tony will find a way to win it."**

**—Former major-league manager Dave Bristol**

TAKING INVENTORY

# THE HALL BY POSITION

**Left fielders**
19

**Shortstops**
23

**Third basemen**
13

**Pitchers**
71

**Catchers**
16

Center fielders
23

Right fielders
23

Second basemen
18

First basemen
21

Designated hitters
1

# PIE TRAYNOR

## THIRD BASEMAN  ELECTED 1948

The only thing Pie Traynor didn't do was hit home runs. Here's what he *did* do as a member of the Pirates from 1920 through 1937:

- Set a still-standing NL record with 2,289 putouts at third base.

- Reached double figures in triples 11 times.

- Drove in more than 100 runs seven times despite never hitting more than a dozen long balls.

- Struck out only 278 times in nearly 2,000 games.

- Walked more than 100 blocks to a World Series game because he never learned to drive.

"If I had to pick the greatest team player in baseball today—and I have some of the greats on my own club—I would have to pick Pie Traynor."

—**John McGraw, manager of the New York Giants**

IMMORTAL MAXIM

"If I'd just tried for them **dinky singles,** I could've batted around **.600.**"

—Babe Ruth

# The Names of Fame

Leo **"The Lip"** Durocher

Mordecai **"Three Finger"** Brown

Reggie **"Mr. October"** Jackson

Babe **"The Sultan of Swat"** Ruth

WILLIE HOWARD MAYS, Jr.
"THE SAY HEY KID"
NEW YORK N.L., SAN FRANCISCO N.L.,
NEW YORK N.L., 1951-1973
ONE OF BASEBALL'S MOST COLORFUL AND
EXCITING STARS. EXCELLED IN ALL PHASES OF
THE GAME. THIRD IN HOMERS (660), RUNS (2,062)
AND TOTAL BASES (6,066); SEVENTH IN HITS
(3,283) AND RBIS (1,903). FIRST TO TOP BOTH
500 HOMERS AND 300 STEALS. LED LEAGUE IN
BATTING ONCE, SLUGGING FIVE TIMES, HOME
RUNS AND STEALS FOUR SEASONS. VOTED N.L.
MVP IN 1954 AND 1965. PLAYED IN 24
ALL-STAR GAMES - A RECORD.

Orlando **"The Baby Bull"** Cepeda

Jimmie **"Double X"** Foxx

Willie **"The Say Hey Kid"** Mays

Lou **"The Iron Horse"** Gehrig

Tony **"Big Doggie"** Perez

LEO ERNEST DUROCHER
"THE LIP"
BROOKLYN, N.L., 1939-1946, 1948
NEW YORK, N.L. 1948-1955
CHICAGO, N.L., 1966-1972
HOUSTON, N.L., 1972-1973
COLORFUL, CONTROVERSIAL MANAGER FOR 24 SEASONS.
WINNING 2,008 GAMES. 7TH ON ALL-TIME LIST.
COMBATIVE, SWASHBUCKLING STYLE A CARRY-OVER
FROM 17 YEARS AS STRONG FIELDING SHORTSTOP FOR
MURDERERS ROW YANKS, GASHOUSE GANG CARDS, REDS
AND DODGERS. MANAGED CLUBS TO PENNANTS IN 1941
AND 1951 AND TO WORLD SERIES WIN IN 1954. 3-TIME
SPORTING NEWS MANAGER OF THE YEAR.

# GEORGE SISLER

**FIRST BASEMAN ● ELECTED 1939**

• Since 1900, no first baseman has ripped more hits or swiped more bases than Sisler, who Ty Cobb once called "the nearest thing to a perfect ballplayer."

• He swatted .407 in 1920 (his 257 hits that season stood as a record for 84 years); .371 in 1921, once ripping ten straight hits; and .420 in 1922, when he compiled a 41-game hitting streak and was the AL MVP.

• Sisler began his career as a left-handed pitcher. He twice beat Walter Johnson and compiled a 2.35 ERA in 24 career games.

# JIM BOTTOMLEY

**FIRST BASEMAN** ⚾ **ELECTED 1974**

A Branch Rickey discovery for the Cardinals, Jim "Sunny" Bottomley was a respected leader, a wonderful hitter, and an even better first baseman. His average was at least .296 the first 11 seasons of his career; he had more RBI than any player in the NL from 1923–1932; and he was the league's 1928 MVP. His virtuoso performances included:

• September 16, 1924: notched a big-league record 12 RBI

• One of two players to have two three-triple games

• July 15, 1927: hit for the cycle on a 5-for-5 day

• One of five players to record two six-hit games

# WHO IN THE HALL...?

1) ...WERE THE ONLY TWO MEMBERS BORN ON CHRISTMAS DAY?

2) ...ARE THE ONLY ENSHRINEES TO STRIKE OUT THE SIDE ON NINE PITCHES TWICE IN A CAREER?

3) ...ONCE PITCHED TWO NINE-INNING COMPLETE GAMES ON THE SAME DAY THREE TIMES IN THE SAME MONTH?

 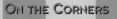

4) ...STOLE SECOND, THIRD, AND HOME IN THE SAME INNING FOUR TIMES?

5) ...WAS THE ONLY FUTURE HALL OF FAMER EVER TO HIT THE FIRST HOME RUN OF HIS CAREER OFF ANOTHER FUTURE MEMBER?

6) ...IS THE ONLY PLAYER TO PLAY EVERY INNING OF EVERY GAME IN A SEASON, STRAIGHT THROUGH THE WORLD SERIES?

1) Pud Galvin and Nellie Fox 2) Lefty Grove, Sandy Koufax, and Nolan Ryan 3) "Iron" Joe McGinnity (winning all six) 4) Ty Cobb 5) Willie Mays, off Warren Spahn on May 28, 1951 6) Cal Ripken, Jr. (of course!) in 1983

# Frank "Home Run" Baker

## THIRD BASEMAN  ELECTED 1955

Frank "Home Run" Baker did many fine things on a baseball diamond, but hitting home runs was not one of them. Wielding a colossal 52-ounce bat, the 170-pound third baseman played in the dead-ball era from 1908–1922, during which he won four straight long ball crowns—but never with more than 12. He retired after reaching his sixth World Series (four with the A's and two with the Yankees), then—as a manager in the low minors—discovered and recommended to Connie Mack a real home run hitter: the legendary Jimmie Foxx.

# TAKING INVENTORY

## HIGHEST PERCENT OF VOTES FOR ELECTION

| | | | |
|---|---|---|---|
| Tom Seaver | 98.84 | Tony Gwynn | 97.61 |
| Nolan Ryan | 98.79 | Mike Schmidt | 96.52 |
| Cal Ripken, Jr. | 98.53 | Johnny Bench | 96.42 |
| Ty Cobb | 98.23 | Steve Carlton | 95.82 |
| George Brett | 98.19 | Babe Ruth | 95.13 |
| Hank Aaron | 97.83 | Honus Wagner | 95.13 |

"**And I want to thank the tremendous fans. We appreciate every boys' group, girls' group, poem, and song. And keep goin' to see the Mets play.**"

—Casey Stengel, 1966

# Bill Terry

**FIRST BASEMAN / MANAGER ⚾ ELECTED 1954**

Perhaps because of his dour personality and tepid relationship with the press, Terry was made to suffer through 15 votes before finally gaining entrance to the Hall. It couldn't have been his credentials. The New York Giants first baseman hit .341 in his career—a modern NL record for left-handed hitters. In 1930, he was the last National Leaguer to swat .400 (.401). Though not a slugger, he knocked home more than 100 runs in six straight seasons. Terry also skippered the Giants for a decade (half as player/manager), winning three pennants and the 1933 World Series.

# St. Louis Cardinals

**If you were the Cardinals manager, wouldn't you like to present this lineup card to the umpire?**

| Catcher | Roger Bresnahan | 1909–1912 |
|---|---|---|
| First Base | Orlando Cepeda | 1966–1968 |
| Second Base | Rogers Hornsby | 1915–1926, 1933 |
| Third Base | John McGraw | 1900 |
| Shortstop | Ozzie Smith | 1982–1996 |
| Outfield | Stan Musial | 1941–1944, 1946–1963 |
| Outfield | Lou Brock | 1964–1979 |
| Outfield | Enos Slaughter | 1938–1942, 1946–1953 |
| Pitcher | Bob Gibson | 1959–1975 |

# ROGER CONNOR

**FIRST BASEMAN / MANAGER**  **ELECTED 1973**

Baseball's original home run hero was not Babe Ruth… it was Roger Connor. For a quarter-century, until Ruth altered the game, this big first baseman held the career record for long balls. One of his 138 home runs came on September 10, 1881, with two outs in the bottom of the ninth and his Troy Trojans trailing by three runs, when Connor muscled up the first recorded grand slam in major-league history. A popular player known as "Dear Old Roger," he once was given a gold watch by fans who took up a collection in the stands.

# WADE BOGGS

## THIRD BASEMAN ᴗ ELECTED 2005

Vision. That was Wade Boggs's secret to winning five
batting titles with the Red Sox (all with averages of
over .350) and walking nearly twice as often as
he struck out. He could read words from
20 feet that most people found blurry at 12.

### "THE CHICKEN MAN'S" SUPERSTITIONS

- ate chicken and cheesecake before
  every game

- for every 7:00 P.M. game, left home at
  1:47 and ran out onto the field at 6:47

- stepped over the foul line going onto
  the field, stepped on it when leaving

- never stood on the mound
  during a conference

- changed his gum when he
  failed to get a hit

"Baseball is just a game, whether it's your second year in Little League or your second year in the big leagues. You should always play the game with **passion,** play the game with **heart.**"

—Wade Boggs, 2005 induction speech

## WHEN BAD THINGS HAPPEN TO GOOD PLAYERS...

In 1907, **Hughie Jennings** was the first player ever ejected from a World Series game.

Bob Gibson served up a home run to the first batter he ever faced—Dodgers rookie Jim Baxes.

Brooks Robinson holds the major-league record for most times hitting into a triple play: four.

Nolan Ryan threw more wild pitches—277—than anyone in history.

# Cooperstown Quiz

**1)** Which two Hall of Famers form the top home run teammate tandem in major-league history?

**2)** Which two Mobile, Alabama–born Hall of Famers both wore No. 44?

**3)** Whose 81-year-old, NL-record 44-game hitting streak did Pete Rose tie in 1978?

**4)** Who holds the major-league record with 24 consecutive pitching wins?

**5)** Which immortal is the only player to have his number retired by Major League Baseball?

**5)** Jackie Robinson, #42
**2)** Hank Aaron and Willie McCovey **3)** Willie Keeler **4)** Carl Hubbell
**1)** Hank Aaron and Eddie Mathews, with 1,267 (863 as teammates)

**"A double play gives you two twenty-sevenths of a baseball game."**

—Casey Stengel

Shortstop Luis Aparicio turns another sparkling double play.

# JACKIE ROBINSON

**SECOND BASEMAN ⚾ ELECTED 1962**

A tacit concurrence that had banned African-Americans from baseball for at least a half-century was scrapped on April 15, 1947, when Jackie Robinson took the field for the Brooklyn Dodgers. And what began with an innocuous 0-for-3 in the box score swelled into a social movement for equality. With serenity in the face of intolerance, dignity in the face of invective, courage in the face of menace, and resolve in the face of cynicism, Robinson exploded the myth of black insufficiency and changed the world. Oh, and by the way, Jackie Robinson played a mean game of baseball. To wit:

- **1947 Rookie of the Year;**
  .297 AVG, 29 SBs

- **1949 NL MVP;**
  .342 AVG, 124 RBI, 37 SBs

- **Six-time All-Star**

- **Played in six World Series**

"You will never know how easy it was for me because of Jackie Robinson."

—Dr. Martin Luther King, Jr.

"Those who tangled with him always admitted afterward he was **a man's man**, a person who would not compromise his convictions."

—Baseball writer Wendell Smith on Robinson, *Baseball Digest*, January 1973

# LUIS APARICIO

Until Ozzie Smith called the question, Aparicio was considered history's greatest defensive shortstop. His leather and wheels keyed the "Go-Go" White Sox of the late '50s and the world-champion Orioles of 1966. Luis almost single-handedly repopularized the stolen base, collecting nearly three times as many as any other AL player from 1956 through 1964.

## "Little Louie's" Records

- Most Games Played at Shortstop: ...................2,581
- Most Consecutive Stolen Base Crowns: .................9
- Most Assists by an AL Shortstop: .....................8,016
- Most Putouts by an AL Shortstop: ....................4,548
- Most Gold Gloves by an AL Shortstop: .......9 (tied)

# NAP LAJOIE

## SECOND BASEMAN / MANAGER  ELECTED 1937

Lajoie was such a respected hitter that, on May 23, 1901, he became the first player we know of to be intentionally walked with the bases loaded. He won the Triple Crown that season and batted .426—a post-1900 record. From 1903 through 1914, including five seasons in which he was Cleveland's player-manager, the club was officially known as the "Naps." The sixth man elected to the Hall, this slick second baseman hit .338 over his 21-year career.

**"[Lajoie] works as noiselessly as a Corliss engine, makes hard plays easy, is great in a pinch, and never gets cold feet."**

**—Evangelist Billy Sunday**

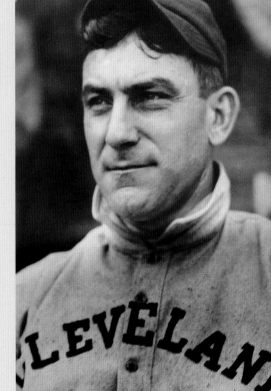

# SATCH vs. JOSH

It was 1942, and the best pitcher in baseball was about to face its finest hitter. Satchel Paige (bottom) of the Kansas City Monarchs bet his buddy Josh Gibson (right) of the Homestead Grays

five bucks that he would strike him out. Not having done so by the seventh inning, Paige unintentionally-intentionally walked two hitters, loading the bases just to get one final crack at the great slugger. Three straight fastballs—three straight strikes. Paige won the battle, but Gibson won the war as his team won.

# JOSH GIBSON

## CATCHER  ELECTED 1972

The "Black Babe Ruth" earned less than one-tenth of the white one's salary—but by most accounts, he hit more home runs. Hailed by anyone who saw him as the most fearsome hitter who ever lived, Gibson routinely hit long balls in excess of 500 feet. In 1936, he went deep 84 times for the Pittsburgh Crawfords. He played the last four seasons of his career with a brain tumor for which he refused surgery. Gibson batted .361 in his final season before dying three months prior to Jackie Robinson's major-league debut.

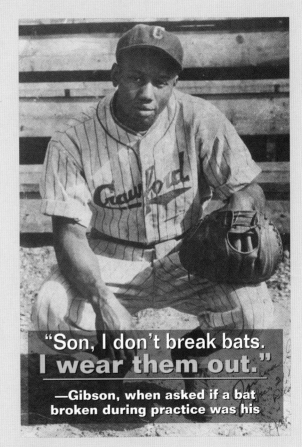

**"Son, I don't break bats. I wear them out."**

—Gibson, when asked if a bat broken during practice was his

# HONUS WAGNER

## SHORTSTOP  ELECTED 1936

Only Babe Ruth has been the central character in more baseball tales than "The Flying Dutchman." There was the time Wagner was about to scoop a grounder when a dog ran onto the field and grabbed the ball—so he picked up the pooch and flipped it to third base for a force play. And the time he caught a pitch from a hotshot pitcher with his bare hand and asked, "Changeup?" And the claim that his swollen-handed first baseman retired rather than catch another throw from the laser-armed shortstop. Whether or not any of those things actually occurred, his stats are 100 percent nonfiction.

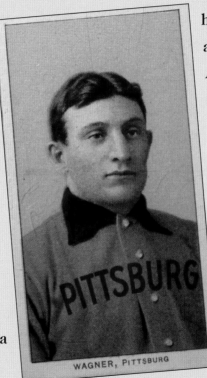

WAGNER, PITTSBURG

- Wagner won eight batting, five RBI, and five stolen base titles.

- He pelted 3,415 hits (eighth all time) and pilfered 722 bases (10th).

- He never hit below .299 from 1897 to 1913.

- He led the Pirates to the 1909 World Series championship.

# BOSTON RED SOX

**If you were the Red Sox manager, wouldn't you like to present this lineup card to the umpire?**

| | | |
|---|---|---|
| Catcher | Carlton Fisk | 1969, 1971–1980 |
| First Base | Jimmie Foxx | 1936–1942 |
| Second Base | Bobby Doerr | 1937–1944, 1946–1951 |
| Third Base | Jimmy Collins | 1895–1907 |
| Shortstop | Joe Cronin | 1935–1945 |
| Outfield | Ted Williams | 1939–1942, 1946–1960 |
| Outfield | Carl Yastrzemski | 1961–1983 |
| Outfield | Tris Speaker | 1907–1915 |
| Pitcher | Cy Young | 1901–1908 |

# JOE MORGAN

**SECOND BASEMAN  ELECTED 1990**

- First player with 200 home runs and 500 stolen bases

- Two-time National League MVP

- Five-time Gold Glove winner

## All-Time Ranks Among Second Basemen

| | | |
|---|---|---|
| Walks | 1st | (1,865) |
| Stolen Bases | 2nd | (689) |
| Home Runs | 4th | (268) |
| Runs | 5th | (1,650) |
| Extra-Base Hits | 6th | (813) |
| Total Bases | 8th | (3,962) |
| Hits | 9th | (2,517) |
| Doubles | 9th | (449) |
| On-Base Pct. | 9th | (.392) |
| RBI | 10th | (1,133) |

# HALL OF FAME GAME

Once every year, in a tradition that dates back to the opening of the Hall of Fame, a major-league exhibition game is held at historic Doubleday Field in Cooperstown. Traditionally, the contest was an interleague affair played on the day following the induction ceremony. Since 2003, however, it has been a stand-alone event at some point during the first half of baseball's regular season. Although today's clubs now often withhold their stars, the likes of everyone from Aaron to Mantle to Williams participated in past contests. The field, which seats 10,000 and measures just 296 feet to left field and 312 to right, usually yields an entertaining offensive display. Proceeds are used for upkeep of the shrine.

*Hank Aaron slams a homer in the 1963 Hall of Fame game.*

# PEE WEE REESE

## SHORTSTOP ⚾ ELECTED 1984

The Red Sox have sold off not one, but two, future Hall of Famers. Nineteen years after shipping Babe Ruth to the Yankees, they sent Pee Wee Reese from their minor-league system to the Dodgers. "The Little Colonel" became the premier NL shortstop of the 1940s and 1950s. He played in seven World Series and made ten All-Star teams.

**"He was the heart and soul of the 'Boys of Summer.' If a player needed to be consoled, Pee Wee would console him. If a player needed to be kicked in the fanny, Pee Wee would do that, too. If a player really needed a friend, Pee Wee was there for him."**

—Famed announcer Vin Scully

# PHIL RIZZUTO

## SHORTSTOP ⚾ ELECTED 1994

On February 2, 1950, the classic TV show *What's My Line?* debuted with its very first "mystery guest"—none other than Phil Rizzuto. Eight months hence, "Scooter's" mug wouldn't have been so hard to recognize; he was the AL MVP. Rizzuto was the shortstop—and spark plug—for seven Yankees World Series–champion teams. What he lacked in size, he made up for in energy and finely honed baseball skills. Later, he undertook a long and colorful broadcasting career in which he popularized the expression "Holy cow!"—not to mention the scorecard symbol "WW" ("Wasn't Watching").

If baseball were ballet, Ozzie would be its Nureyev. Playing shortstop with an athletic grace previously inconceivable, he carved a unique path to Cooperstown as perhaps the all-time foremost practitioner of defense—at any position. He still holds positional records for assists, double plays, and Gold Gloves (13). "The Wizard of Oz" evolved to create offense, as well. He is one of only four players (including Cooperstown peers Ty Cobb, Eddie Collins, and Max Carey) with at least 2,000 hits, 1,000 walks, 200 sacrifices, and 500 stolen bases.

"**When you look at Dorothy's journey down the Yellow Brick Road and her three delightful companions—the scarecrow, the tin man, and the cowardly lion—you will find the exact same road map as I found in the baseball.**"

—Ozzie "The Wizard of Oz" Smith, in his 2002 induction speech, while holding a sliced-open baseball

# JOHNNY BENCH

**CATCHER ✵ ELECTED 1989**

Johnny set a "benchmark"
for catchers in the following
categories:

- Intelligence: High school
  valedictorian
- Toughness: Endured
  10 broken bones in his feet
- Durability: Tied a record
  with 100-plus games caught
  in 13 straight seasons
- Power: Second-most
  homers ever by an NL
  catcher (327; 389 overall)
- Defense: Catchers-record
  10 straight Gold Gloves
- Clutch Bat: Homered in 9
  of 10 postseason series;
  1976 World Series MVP

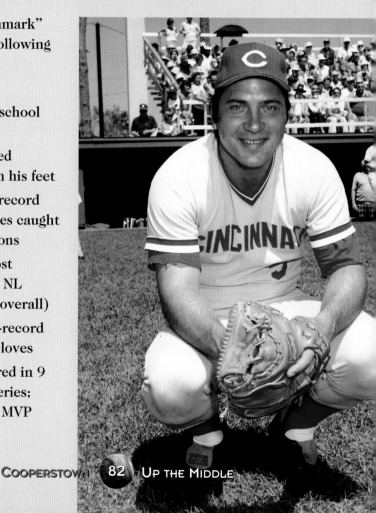

"I don't want to embarrass any catcher by comparing them to Johnny Bench."

—Sparky Anderson

# LOU BOUDREAU

**SHORTSTOP / MANAGER ● ELECTED 1970**

An elite shortstop in the 1940s, Boudreau was named to all but two All-Star teams in that decade. He won the 1944 AL batting crown with a mark of .327, but his greatest year was 1948, when he was voted MVP after setting career highs in the Triple Crown stats (.355–18–106) for the world-champion Indians. In 1942, he was named Cleveland's player-manager—earning the nickname "The Boy Manager" by becoming, at 24, the youngest-ever skipper to open a season.

# ROD CAREW

**SECOND BASEMAN / FIRST BASEMAN**  **ELECTED 1991**

Former White Sox infielder Alan Bannister said of Carew, "He's the only guy I know who can go 4-for-3." Indeed, there have been few better at the art of the base hit. An All-Star in 18 consecutive seasons (1967–1984), Carew won seven batting titles for the Twins, including in 1977, when he hit .388 as the AL MVP. He was also a swift and crafty baserunner who stole 353 bags in his career, including home seven times in 1969.

# "COUNTRY" HARDBALL

In the 1909 World Series, the two best players in the game—arguably two of the five best *ever*—went head-to-head, and something had to give. In one exchange, the Tigers' parochial Georgian Ty Cobb, standing on first base, supposedly bellowed to Pirates shortstop Honus "The Flying Dutchman" Wagner: "I'm coming down on the next pitch, Krauthead!" "I'll be waiting," Wagner snapped

TY COBB, Detroit        HANS WAGNER, Pittsburg

back. Cobb did indeed come, and Wagner knocked out two of his teeth with a hard "out" tag on the attempted steal. Pittsburgh won the series in seven games, with Wagner definitively outplaying Cobb.

# Cooperstown Quiz

**1)** Which Hall of Fame outfielder was drafted in three pro sports?

**2)** Name the two Hall of Famers known most commonly as "Lefty."

**3)** Who was the first catcher ever voted NL Rookie of the Year?

**4)** Which "Little" shortstop was the first Venezuelan elected to the Hall?

**5)** Which Chicago Cubs great was the first player to jump directly from the Negro Leagues to the majors?

**1)** Dave Winfield (by the San Diego Padres, the NFL's Minnesota Vikings, and the NBA's Atlanta Hawks and the ABA's Utah Stars) **2)** Grove and Gomez **3)** Johnny Bench **4)** "Little Louie" Aparicio **5)** Ernie Banks

# LUKE APPLING

### SHORTSTOP  ELECTED 1964

White Sox fans once voted shortstop Luke Appling the greatest player in their team's history. He made a strong case in the 1930s and 1940s. Here's how "Old Aches and Pains" ranked on the franchise leaderboards through 2007:

| | | |
|---|---|---|
| **At-Bats** | 1st | 8,856 |
| **Average** | 7th | .310 |
| **Doubles** | 2nd | 440 |
| **Extra-Base Hits** | 2nd | 587 |
| **Games** | 1st | 2,422 |
| **Hits** | 1st | 2,749 |
| **On-Base Pct.** | 4th | .399 |
| **RBI** | 2nd | 1,116 |
| **Runs** | 2nd | 1,319 |
| **Singles** | 1st | 2,162 |
| **Total Bases** | 2nd | 3,528 |
| **Triples** | 3rd | 102 |
| **Walks** | 2nd | 1,302 |

# ROBIN YOUNT

**SHORTSTOP / OUTFIELDER** 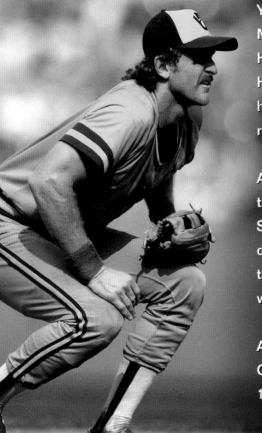 **ELECTED 1999**

Yount played 20 seasons for the Milwaukee Brewers (1974–93). He, Willie Mays, and Rickey Henderson are the only players in history with 3,000 hits, 250 home runs, and 250 stolen bases.

As a shortstop in 1982, he swept the AL MVP, Gold Glove, and Silver Slugger Awards. As an outfielder in 1989, he was again the MVP and Silver Slugger winner.

Although his Brewers lost to the Cardinals, Robin hit .414 in the 1982 World Series.

# EDDIE COLLINS

 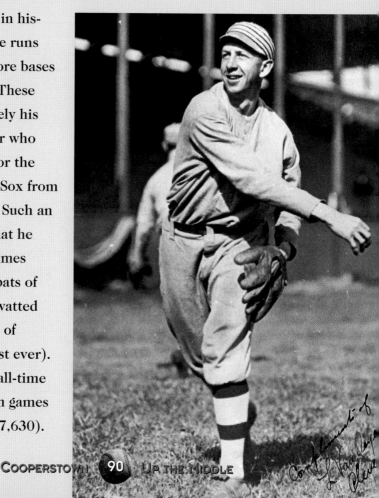

No second baseman in history has scored more runs (1,821) or stolen more bases (744) than Collins. These stats indicate precisely his legacy as a ballplayer who made it all happen for the Athletics and White Sox from 1906 through 1930. Such an amazing batsmith that he struck out only 29 times in the last 1,068 at-bats of his career, Collins swatted .333 on the strength of 3,315 hits (10th-most ever). "Cocky" is also the all-time second base leader in games (2,650) and assists (7,630).

# CAL RIPKEN, JR.

## SHORTSTOP ● ELECTED 2007

- Established a Hall of Fame voting record by being named on 537 ballots, breaking the previous mark of 491 by Nolan Ryan in 1999. Ripken's percentage of 98.53 percent is the third highest behind Tom Seaver (98.83 in 1992) and Nolan Ryan (98.79 in 1999).

- Played in a record 2,632 straight games, spanning 16 seasons from May 30, 1982, to September 20, 1998, for the Baltimore Orioles, breaking the 56-year-old record set by the "Iron Horse" Lou Gehrig.

- Elected to start more All-Star Games (17) than any other player.

- Is the only American League shortstop to win two MVP Awards.

- Has more seasons of 50 extra-base hits (12) than any other shortstop.

# CARLTON FISK

**CATCHER • ELECTED 2000**

The only catcher ever to hit more home runs than Fisk is Mike Piazza, but there's one homer for which Fisk is best remembered. In the 12th inning of Game 6 of the 1975 World Series, he frantically "waved" fair his blast that beat the Reds. Almost unbelievably, the ball hit the foul pole and bounced fair, winning the game.

How tough was "Pudge"? He caught more games than any catcher in history despite this litany of injuries:

- Broken arm
- Two broken hands
- Knee damage
- Cracked ribs
- Separated shoulder

## PUT ME IN, COACH

"I had too much respect for the game to play it any other way, and if there was a single reason I am here today, it is because of one word, respect. I love to play baseball."

—Ryne Sandberg, in his 2005 induction speech

NATIONAL

NATIONAL

# WHO IN THE HALL...?

1) ...are the only three players to hit safely in seven consecutive All-Star Games?

2) ...holds the record for having his team shut out the most times in his pitching starts?

3) ...named his son after his Hall of Fame double-play partner?

4) ...hit five career home runs in 1-0 games (the most in history)?

5) ...hit major-league home runs off two former NBA players?

6) ...pitched the first perfect game in the modern era (May 5, 1904)?

**1)** Mickey Mantle, Joe Morgan, and Dave Winfield **2)** Walter Johnson, 65 **3)** Luis Aparicio named his son Nelson after White Sox teammate Nellie Fox **4)** Ted Williams **5)** Harmon Killebrew, off Dave DeBusschere and Gene Conley **6)** Cy Young

# BON VOYAGE

One would think that if five straight 100-RBI seasons did not make a player secure with his team, marrying the owner's niece would. Joe Cronin held both of those distinctions in 1934, but Washington traded the great shortstop to the Red Sox just a year after the wedding.

# MICKEY COCHRANE

CATCHER  ELECTED 1947

Cochrane's .320 career batting average is the highest all-time among catchers. He never won a batting title, but he topped .300 nine times in 13 seasons.

The fiery "Black Mike" was named the American League MVP in 1928 and again in 1934.

He played in five World Series, winning with the 1929 and 1930 Athletics, as well as with the 1935 Tigers as their player-manager.

As Mutt Mantle's favorite player, he was the namesake for Mutt's son, Mickey.

# HALL OF FAME FOLLIES

# WHEN BAD THINGS HAPPEN TO GOOD PLAYERS . . .

Honus Wagner struck out to end the very first World Series in 1903.

Walter Johnson holds a record by hitting batters with a pitch 206 times.

An Orlando police officer threatened to arrest Kirby Puckett ▼ if he kept hitting balls that dented cars and broke windshields outside the Twins' spring training ballpark.

Jim Palmer ▲ is the only pitcher ever to allow three home runs in an All-Star Game (1977).

Phil Niekro is the only pitcher ever to lead his league in runs allowed three times.

# CHARLIE GEHRINGER

## SECOND BASEMAN ● ELECTED 1949

Charlie Gehringer— nicknamed "The Mechanical Man" by Lefty Gomez because of his detached personality and robotic consistency— missed his Hall of Fame induction ceremony. He was busy getting hitched. Charlie also did a three-year hitch in the Navy after he retired with a 1937 MVP Award and an assortment of AL leaderships in runs, hits, doubles, triples, batting average, and second base fielding on his resume.

"He says hello on opening day and good-bye on closing day, and in between he hits .350."

—Mickey Cochrane

# YOGI BERRA

**CATCHER ⚬ ELECTED 1972**

Behind the fractured quotations, behind the cartoonish name, behind the clunky appearance, Yogi Berra was a ballplayer's ballplayer, a shrewd manager, a successful businessman—and the greatest winner in the history of the game. In all

## Yogi's World Series Career Records

- Most Series Played In: ......14
- Most Series Won: ...............10
- Most Games: ..........................75
- Most Hits: ...............................71
- Most Doubles: .........10 (tied)

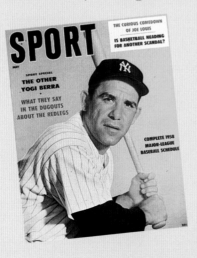

but five of his 19 seasons, he ended up in the World Series—capturing three American League MVP Awards and making 15 consecutive All-Star teams for the Yankees along the way. As a manager, Berra won a pennant in each league.

"He seemed to be doing everything wrong, yet everything came out right. **He stopped everything behind the plate** and **hit everything in front of it.**"

**—Mel Ott**

# CHICAGO CUBS

**If you were the Cubs manager, wouldn't you like to present this lineup card to the umpire?**

| | | |
|---|---|---|
| Catcher | Gabby Hartnett | 1922–1940 |
| First Base | Cap Anson | 1876–1897 |
| Second Base | Ryne Sandberg | 1981–1994, 1996–1997 |
| Third Base | Freddie Lindstrom | 1935 |
| Shortstop | Ernie Banks | 1953–1971 |
| Outfield | Billy Williams | 1959–1974 |
| Outfield | Hack Wilson | 1926–1931 |
| Outfield | Ralph Kiner | 1953–1954 |
| Pitcher | Ferguson Jenkins | 1966–1973, 1982–1983 |

# ERNIE BANKS

In 1977, Banks received a license plate from the state of Illinois that was as evocative as the back of any baseball card: MR CUB, it read. The epitome of the humility and enthusiasm that is meant to characterize the game, Ernie hit 512 home runs in his 19 Windy City seasons.

## "Let's Play 2"

- 2 NL MVP Awards
- 2 NL Home Run Titles
- 2 NL RBI Crowns
- 2-Position All-Star (SS, 1B)

# The Names of Fame

LLOYD JAMES WANER
"LITTLE POISON"
PITTSBURGH N.L., BOSTON N.L.,
CINCINNATI N.L., PHILADELPHIA N.L.,
BROOKLYN N.L. 1927-1945
MADE 223 HITS IN 1927 FIRST YEAR
WITH PITTSBURGH INCLUDING 198 SINGLES,
A MODERN MAJOR LEAGUE RECORD.
LED N.L. IN MOST SINGLES 1927-1928-1929-1931.
LIFE TOTAL 2459 HITS. BATTING AVERAGE .316.
WITH BROTHER PAUL "BIG POISON"
STARRED IN PITTSBURGH OUTFIELD
1927-1940

John **"Little Napoleon"** McGraw

Joe **"Ducky"** Medwick

Johnny **"The Big Cat"** Mize

Ernie **"Schnozz"** Lombardi

Connie **"The Tall Tactician"** Mack

**"Sliding Billy"** Hamilton

Luke **"Old Aches and Pains"** Appling

Enos **"Country"** Slaughter

Lloyd **"Little Poison"** Waner

Paul **"Big Poison"** Waner

PAUL GLEE WANER
(BIG POISON)
PITTSBURGH-BROOKLYN-BOSTON, N.L.,
NEW YORK, A.L.
1926-1945
LEFT HANDED HITTING OUTFIELDER BATTED
.300 OR BETTER 14 TIMES IN NATIONAL
LEAGUE. ONE OF SEVEN PLAYERS EVER TO
COMPILE 3,000 OR MORE HITS. SET MODERN
N.L. RECORD BY COLLECTING 200 OR MORE
HITS EIGHT SEASONS. MOST VALUABLE PLAYER
IN 1927 AND FOUR TIMES SELECTED FOR
ALL STAR GAME.

# BILL DICKEY

## CATCHER / MANAGER · ELECTED 1954

Although he won neither a major award nor a statistical title, Dickey's body of work is imposing. During the span of his career, 1928–46, no catcher amassed more hits (1,969), RBI (1,209), or home runs (202). The 11-time All-Star was a quiet key to seven Yankees world championships.

**"A catcher must want to catch.** He must make up his mind that it isn't the terrible job it is painted, and that he isn't going to say every day, 'Why, oh why, with so many other positions in baseball, did I take up this one?'"

—Dickey

"People ask me what I do in winter when there's no baseball. I'll tell you what I do. I stare out the window and **wait for spring.**"

—Hornsby

# ROGERS HORNSBY

## SECOND BASEMAN / SHORTSTOP / THIRD BASEMAN / MANAGER
### ⚾ ELECTED 1942

If "Rajah" wasn't the greatest hitter who ever laced 'em up, he was close.
Check this out:

| | Hornsby | Ruth | Cobb | Williams | Wagner | Bonds |
|---|---|---|---|---|---|---|
| .300 Seasons* | 19 | 17 | 23 | 18 | 16 | 11 |
| .400 Seasons* | 4 | 0 | 3 | 3 | 0 | 0 |
| Batting Titles | 7 | 1 | 11 | 6 | 8 | 2 |
| On-Base Pct. Titles | 9 | 10 | 7 | 12 | 4 | 9 |
| Slug. Pct. Titles | 9 | 13 | 8 | 9 | 6 | 7 |
| RBI Titles | 4 | 6 | 4 | 4 | 5 | 1 |
| 150-Hit Seasons | 13 | 11 | 18 | 10 | 16 | 7 |
| MVPs | 2 | 1 | 1 | 2 | n/a | 7 |
| Triple Crowns | 2 | 0 | 1 | 2 | 0 | 0 |

* Includes partial seasons

"I've got 12 pages here. That's not like me. I'll probably skip half of it and get halfway through this thing and quit anyhow. It's getting awful hot out here.... So, but anyhow, I think defense belongs in the Hall of Fame.... This is gonna be hard, so I probably won't say about half of this stuff.... I think you can kiss these 12 pages down the drain.... I want to thank all the friends and family that made this long trip up here to listen to me speak and hear this crap.... Thanks everybody. That's enough."

—A "speechless" Bill Mazeroski, never much one for high-falootin' verbiage, at his 2001 induction

COOPERSTOWN 108 UP THE MIDDLE

WILLIAM STANLEY MAZ
"MAZ"

# BILL MAZEROSKI

## SECOND BASEMAN ❧ ELECTED 2001

"Maz" hit a modest .260 and averaged eight homers a year in his career, but he set the standard for defensive play at second base and hit one of the most dramatic home runs in baseball history. An eight-time Gold Glover, his numerous records for the position include most career double plays with 1,706. In Game 7 of the 1960 World Series, he hacked at a ninth-inning slider from the Yankees' Ralph Terry and ended the Pirates' 35-year title drought with the first-ever Series-ending homer.

# GARY CARTER

Just weeks after his young mother died of leukemia, a 12-year-old Gary Carter pitched a no-hitter in Little League. That same grit defined his major-league catching career—and defied his image as the ever-smiling, silver-tongued, pretty-boy Southern Californian that earned him the nickname "The Kid." Carter won three Gold Gloves and five Silver Slugger Awards, blasted 324 homers, and topped 100 RBI on four occasions. Always a magnet for the "moment," he twice was an All-Star Game MVP, and for the world-champ 1986 Mets, he delivered 16 game-winning hits and several postseason heroics.

# JOE CRONIN

**SHORTSTOP / MANAGER**  **ELECTED 1956**

## ON THE DIAMOND

He was a seven-time All-Star shortstop; he hit .346 with 126 RBI in 1930; and he posted eight .300 and 100-RBI seasons. He is the only American Leaguer to pinch-hit home runs in both games of a double-header; he was runner-up for the 1933 AL MVP award; and he shares AL records with 13 hits in a three-game span and 15 in four.

## OFF THE DIAMOND

He married the niece of Senators owner Clark Griffith, who then sold him to the Red Sox, and he managed the Washington Senators for two years and Boston for 13. As the Red Sox GM, he passed up a chance to sign a 16-year-old Negro Leaguer by the name of Willie Mays. He was president of the American League from 1959 to 1973.

# BILLY HERMAN

There are no stats for "bat-handling," but Billy Herman probably executed as many successful hit-and-run plays and moved as many runners as anyone did. His stats weren't bad either. Primarily for the Cubs and Dodgers from 1931–1947, he batted .304, tagged at least 30 doubles 11 times, and played in 10 All-Star Games and four World Series. He still ranks among the NL's all-time top five second basemen in assists, putouts, and DPs.

Herman also has this unique distinction: He is the only player ever removed from an All-Star Game and then reinserted, which happened in 1934 when his replacement, Frankie Frisch, was injured.

# ARKY VAUGHAN

**SHORTSTOP** ⚾ **ELECTED 1985**

If a Hall of Famer can be underrated, that was Vaughan's fate. He hit .300 or better in 11 of his 12 seasons as a regular for the Pirates and Dodgers, including .385 as the 1935 NL batting champ. A true table-setter, he led the league in on-base percentage, runs, and triples three times apiece. Alas, four years after he retired in 1948, Arky drowned trying to save a friend.

> "I never saw anybody who could go from first to third or from second to home faster than Vaughan. Like we used to say, when he went around second his hip pocket was dipping sand. That's how sharp he cut those corners."
>
> —Rip Sewell

# MAGIC NUMBERS

**12** Ground rule doubles in the first game Hank Aaron ever played because of ball bouncing into temporary seating (Aaron went 0-for-5.)

**45.8** Percent of all Phillies wins (27 of 59) — a modern record — by Steve Carlton in 1972

**465** Starts by Don Drysdale under Walter Alston, a record for a pitcher-manager pair

**577,610** Dollars paid for Shoeless Joe Jackson's "Black Betsy" bat in 2002

**301** Home runs by Rogers Hornsby, the most ever by a hitter who never played in an All-Star Game

# WHO IN THE HALL...?

**1) IS THE ONLY PLAYER EVER TO GET FIVE HITS IN HIS FIRST NINE-INNING MAJOR LEAGUE GAME?**

**2) HOLDS THE RECORD FOR MOST OPENING DAY PITCHING STARTS?**

**3) WAS THE SECOND AFRICAN-AMERICAN ELECTED?**

**4) WERE THE TWO PLAYERS WHO REACHED THE 3,000-HIT AND 300-WIN MILESTONES ON THE SAME DAY?**

**5) IS THE ONLY PLAYER TO HAVE 2,000 HITS AND 100 PITCHING VICTORIES?**

**1)** Fred Clarke on June 30, 1894 **2)** Tom Seaver, 16 **3)** Roy Campanella **4)** Rod Carew and Tom Seaver on August 4, 1985 **5)** John Ward

# Cooperstown Quiz

1) Who was the first African-American network TV baseball broadcaster?

2) Who was the youngest player elected to the Hall of Fame?

3) Who was the first Hispanic player elected to the Hall of Fame?

4) Who homered in his first at-bat in the first game he ever managed?

5) Who was the only shortstop to lead the majors in home runs between 1901 and 2001?

1) Jackie Robinson (for ABC) in 1965 2) Sandy Koufax, 36 3) Roberto Clemente in 1973 4) Player-manager Frank Robinson, April 8, 1975 5) Ernie Banks, in 1958 and 1960

# ROY CAMPANELLA

## CATCHER ⚾ ELECTED 1969

"Campy" was the game's first African-American catcher and the second African-American to be elected to the Hall of Fame. A member of the Negro National League by age 15, he had to wait 10 seasons for the major-league doors to swing open to blacks. The three-time NL MVP led the Brooklyn Dodgers to five pennants and, in 1955, their first world title.

> **"You gotta be a man to play baseball for a living, but you gotta have a lot of little boy in you, too."**
>
> —Campanella

# CHAPTER THREE

# CAN O' CORN

> ## "The secret to my success was clean living and a fast-moving outfield."
>
> —Hall of Fame pitcher
> Lefty Gomez

Lefty Gomez (left) chats with Lou Gehrig (center) and Jimmie Foxx before the start of the 1939 All-Star Game.

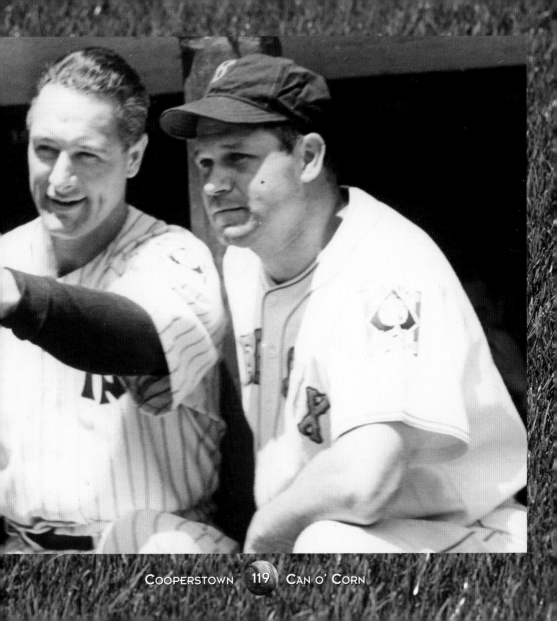

# WILLIE MAYS

**OUTFIELDER** • **ELECTED 1979**

If one were to build the perfect ballplayer, the assemblage might well start with Willie Mays's batting skills...and speed...and defense...and instincts...and guts. It has been said that he was made to play the game, but it was almost as if the game was made for him. "The Say Hey Kid" did it all.

**Hitting:** 660 home runs • .302 batting average • 3,283 hits • Top 10 all time in homers, total bases, runs, and extra-base hits • Led NL in slugging five times.

**Running:** 338 stolen bases, with four league titles • First two 30-homer/30-steal seasons in NL history.

**Defense:** 12 Gold Gloves, tying a record for outfielders • MLB outfield-record 7,095 putouts • Made "The Catch" that turned the tide of the 1954 World Series for the Giants.

"If somebody came up and hit .450, stole 100 bases, and performed a miracle in the field every day, I'd still look you in the eye and say **Willie was better.**"

—Leo Durocher

 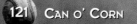

# HACK WILSON

**OUTFIELDER  ELECTED 1979**

- Holds the all-time single-season RBI record with 191 for the 1930 Cubs.

- Amassed 64 more home runs and 94 more RBI than any other player from 1926 through 1930, winning four home run crowns.

- Stood only 5'6", yet weighed nearly 200 pounds. Saw his career flame out prematurely for reasons attributed to alcohol and depression.

# MEL OTT

The first player in NL annals to reach 500 home runs stood a mere 5´9˝ tall. Employing a unique leg kick that would drive today's batting instructors batty, the Giants' Mel Ott generated enough oomph to hit an amazing 202 more homers than anyone in his league between 1929 and 1945. The affable "Master Melvin" was named to 12 straight All-Star teams.

# KIRBY PUCKETT

**OUTFIELDER ᛝ ELECTED 2001**

A firepluggish, talent-crammed physique and a carbonated personality made "Puck" one of the most popular players of recent times. His career included 2,304 hits and a half-dozen Silver Slugger and Gold Glove awards apiece—plus post-season heroics that carried the Twins to a pair of world titles (1987 and 1991). Kirby's career and life ended far too soon—at age 35 by glaucoma and at 45 by a stroke, respectively.

## "Something about the guy just makes you **feel good.**"

**—Tom Kelly, Puckett's manager**

# TONY GWYNN

OUTFIELDER ● ELECTED 2007

- Owns a career batting average of .338, which is better than any player since Ted Williams's .344.

- Hit .350 or better five years in a row—a streak unmatched by any hitter since Rogers Hornsby.

- Won eight batting titles, tying Honus Wagner's record for the most in National League history.

- Finished in the top 10 in the batting race in every full season of his career and finished in the top five in all but two.

- Was a 15-time All-Star and won five Gold Gloves.

# JOE DiMAGGIO

A true American icon, DiMaggio augmented his exceptional skills with a gracious manner and charisma that wouldn't quit. Playing on nine World Series–winning Yankee teams, he was an All-Star in every one of his 13 seasons and captured three MVP Awards and two league leaderships apiece in each Triple Crown stat.

## "56"

On the short list of records likely never to be broken is Joltin' Joe's 56-game hitting streak of 1941. No one else has topped 44. Ted Williams, who won the Triple Crown that year, nevertheless lost the MVP Award to DiMaggio, conceding magnanimously, "I believe there isn't a record in the books that will be harder to break than Joe's 56 games. It may be the greatest batting achievement of all."

"There was never a day when I was as good as Joe DiMaggio at his best. Joe was the best, the very best I ever saw."

—Stan Musial

 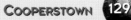

# PITTSBURGH PIRATES

**If you were the Pirates manager, wouldn't you like to present this lineup card to the umpire?**

| | | |
|---|---|---|
| **Catcher** | **Al Lopez** | 1940–1946 |
| **First Base** | **Jake Beckley** | 1888–1889, 1891–1896 |
| **Second Base** | **Bill Mazeroski** | 1956–1972 |
| **Third Base** | **Pie Traynor** | 1920–1937 |
| **Shortstop** | **Honus Wagner** | 1900–1907 |
| **Outfield** | **Roberto Clemente** | 1955–1972 |
| **Outfield** | **Willie Stargell** | 1962–1982 |
| **Outfield** | **Ralph Kiner** | 1946–1953 |
| **Pitcher** | **Pud Galvin** | 1887–1889, 1891–1892 |

# OSCAR CHARLESTON

**OUTFIELDER / FIRST BASEMAN / MANAGER  ELECTED 1976**

There is no shortage of support for Charleston as the most complete—if not the greatest—of all Negro Leaguers. For 40 years, he played for and/or managed numerous clubs with the hitting facility, speed, outfield brilliance, and even the fierce temperament of a Ty Cobb. Fearless and proud, he once ripped the hood off a Klansman and dared him to converse face-to-face. Charleston is believed to have compiled a lifetime batting average of higher than .350, including a .445 campaign in the Eastern Colored League.

# STAN MUSIAL

## OUTFIELDER / FIRST BASEMAN ⚬ ELECTED 1969

When Musial retired in 1963, he owned more extra-base hits than any player in history (only Hank Aaron and Barry Bonds have passed him since), as well as National League records for RBI and hits.

Musial, who was invited to 24 All-Star Games in 20 seasons, captured three MVP Awards, seven batting crowns, and three World Series titles with the Cardinals.

Stan earned the nickname "The Man" because of his well-mannered comportment, devotion to community and family, and unfailingly pleasant demeanor.

### MAN, OH MAN!

- Posted an 18-win season as a minor-league pitcher.

- Ripped 1,815 hits at home and 1,815 hits on the road.

- Missed the 1948 Triple Crown by one homer.

- Asked for and received a 20 percent pay cut in 1960 because he'd batted only .255 the year before.

"Here stands baseball's perfect warrior. Here stands baseball's perfect knight."

—Commissioner Ford Frick upon Musial's retirement

# POINTED COMMENTS

Three things Babe Ruth had to say about his "called shot" in Game 3 of the 1932 World Series:

"I'm going to knock the next pitch right down your throat."

"Go get the ball and I'll autograph it for you."
— to first baseman Charlie Grimm as he circled the bases

"It was the funniest, proudest moment I ever had in baseball."

# ED DELAHANTY

"Big Ed" Delahanty was a three-time .400 hitter and two-time NL home run champ for the 19th-century Phillies. His resume also included a pair of six-hit games, a streak of ten consecutive hits, and a four-home run contest.

It ended abruptly for the notoriously rowdy 35-year-old: In the middle of the 1903 season, he got kicked off a train for trying to haul a sleeping woman out of her berth by the ankles. Delahanty's whereabouts were unknown for days before his body was recovered from the Niagara River. Whether he jumped, was pushed, or fell in a drunken stupor has never been determined.

# AL KALINE

## IF....

...Al had not broken his collarbone, hand, and arm—and if he had hit just one more homer—he would have been the first American Leaguer with 400 bombs and 3,000 hits.

...he had gotten 23 more hits, he would have swatted .300 for his career.

...Kaline had squeezed out two more doubles, he would have ended up with 500.

...one more Gold Glove had come his way, he'd be the sole leader of AL outfielders, with 11.

# CHUCK KLEIN

Chuck Klein was an MVP and two-time runner-up; he won a Triple Crown; he drove in 170 runs in a season; he held the NL extra-base hit record of 107 for 71 years; and—until the Indians' Grady Sizemore did it in 2006—he was the only man to combine 50 doubles, 10 triples, 20 homers, and 20 steals in one campaign. Amazingly, he accomplished every one of those things in a five-year period (1929–1934). After that, undermined by injuries and a move away from Philadelphia's 280-foot right-field line, his stats went into a freefall. As a result, it took nearly two decades for Klein's plaque to be hung in Cooperstown—but it's an impressive read.

"Trying to throw a fastball by Henry Aaron is like trying to **sneak a sunrise past a rooster.**"

—Pitcher Curt Simmons

# HANK AARON

## OUTFIELDER ⚬ ELECTED 1982

The greatest home run hitter who ever lived never clouted more than 47 in a season. His coaches regularly tried to tinker with a swing afflicted with a hitch, a grip that was untraditional, a style in which he hit off the wrong foot, and an approach that was a tad impatient. He didn't hit the ball for tape-measure distances, or stand and admire his drives, or blow kisses to ghosts, or point to the sky. Henry Louis Aaron simply hit the ball hard and often for a very long time.

Here is a partial list of things Aaron did that no one else has done before or since:

- Hammered 755 home runs

- Amassed 1,000 RBI on homers and 1,000 on other hits

- Collected 6,856 total bases

- Drove in 2,297 runs

- Smacked 1,477 extra-base hits

- Hit 20 or more homers in 20 consecutive seasons

- Collected 80 RBI in 18 different seasons

# TRIS SPEAKER

Had there been such a thing as a Gold Glove early in the 20th century, Speaker would have run out of room in his trophy case. The Red Sox and Indians star, known for playing shallow, was regarded as the best center fielder ever seen by the likes of everyone from Ty Cobb to Shoeless Joe Jackson. Speaker is by far the all-time leader in outfield assists (449) and double plays (139). He could hit, too:

## All-Time Rankings

Doubles.....................1st (792)

Hits .........................5th (3,514)

Batting Average......6th (.345)

Triples ......................6th (222)

Runs.....................11th (1,882)

On-Base Pct...........12th (.428)

# SAM CRAWFORD

**OUTFIELDER ⚜ ELECTED 1957**

Until Mark McGwire came along, Crawford was the only man to win home run crowns in both leagues—with the modest totals of 16 for the 1901 Reds and seven for the 1908 Tigers. But triples are what "Wahoo Sam" was really about.

- His 309 triples are a career record.

- He hit at least 10 in each of his 17 full seasons.

- He led his league six times.

- He would have had more— if he hadn't stretched 51 of them into inside-the-park home runs.

# SWEET REVENGE

Folks cringed when, in 1973, Reggie Jackson bewailed his lack of notoriety in Oakland. "If I played [in New York], they'd name a candy bar after me," he declared. Four years later that's exactly what happened. Pundits had a field day with the swaggering slugger. One wrote that the peanut, caramel, and chocolate confection was the only candy bar that tasted like a hot dog. Fellow immortal Catfish Hunter mocked, "When you unwrap a Reggie Bar, it tells you how good it is." But Jackson had the last laugh, reaching three World Series in five years with the Yankees, once by beating Oakland in the playoffs.

REGGIE!®

NET WT. 1.5 OZ.
(42 g)

Chocolaty covered caramel and peanuts

One of baseball's most enigmatic figures, Jackson elevated two characteristics to an art form: brazen self-promotion and an unfailing ability to rise to the moment. His greatest achievements:

- Hitting home runs on four consecutive swings in the 1977 World Series.

- Batting .360 in two Fall Classics, one for the A's and one for the Yankees.

- Winning four home run crowns and retiring with 563.

"THERE IS **NO ONE** WHO DOES AS MANY THINGS AS WELL AS I DO."

—JACKSON

# HARRY HEILMANN

## OUTFIELDER / INFIELDER  ELECTED 1952

Heilmann is one of only four players to hit better than .390 four times. In each instance, he won the AL batting title—but it took him until the season's final day to secure the last two. An inelegant outfielder dubbed "Slug," he swatted .360 from 1919 to 1929 for the Tigers. Sidebars to Heilmann's career are that he dove into the Detroit River to save a drowning woman in 1916; he sold a $50,000 life insurance policy to Babe Ruth in 1923; and he died in 1951 under the erroneous impression he'd already been elected to the Hall of Fame. (He was elected the following year.)

# GIVE 'EM HELL, HARRY

Many fans know the story of how Ted Williams refused to protect his .400 batting average by sitting out the last day of the 1941 season, then went 6-for-8 in a doubleheader. Perhaps his inspiration was Harry Heilmann. In 1925's final month, the Tigers outfielder stormed from 50 points behind Tris Speaker to challenge for the AL batting title. Prior to a season-ending twin bill, Heilmann trailed, .38826 to Speaker's .38927. He nudged ahead of the inactive Speaker by .0002 after the first game but insisted on playing the nightcap, in which he went 3-for-3 to finish at .393.

# MICKEY MANTLE

## OUTFIELDER ⚜ ELECTED 1974

Twelve players have hit more home runs than Mickey Mantle. Nearly 50 have driven in more runs. He soon will fall out of the top 100 in hits. But it is debatable whether anyone was a better all-around ballplayer than "The Mick" in his prime—and unlikely that any was more popular. Defying "counter-productive" personal habits, injuries, and disease that would have rendered more docile competitors useless, the great Yankee:

- Won three MVP Awards and the 1956 Triple Crown.

- Made 16 All-Star teams in his 18 seasons.

- Hit a record 18 home runs for 12 World Series teams (seven of them champions).

- Set records for homers (536), on-base percentage (.421), and walks (1,733) by a switch-hitter.

- Pulverized a pitch on September 10, 1960, that was listed in the *Guinness Book of World Records* as having traveled 643 feet.

**Nobody** is half as good as Mickey Mantle."

—Al Kaline, responding to a young boy who had said to him, "You're not half as good as Mickey Mantle."

"You're going to be a **great player**, kid."

—Jackie Robinson to a 20-year-old Mantle in 1952

# MAGIC NUMBERS

**3** 1–0 shutouts by Babe Ruth over Walter Johnson before he gave up pitching.

**5** Home runs on his birthday by Al Simmons—a record.

**9** Future Hall of Famers in the Red Sox–Yankees contest of April 20, 1939—the only time Lou Gehrig and Ted Williams played in the same game.

**22** Career extra-inning home runs, a record, by Willie Mays.

**121** RBI by Hughie Jennings in 1896, a record for a player without a single home run.

# WILLIE KEELER

Hitting, said "Wee Willie," was simple: "Hit 'em where they ain't." One of history's great singles hitters, bunters, and leadoff pests, the 5´4˝, 140-pound right fielder was a magician with the bat. His favorite tactic was choking up more than a foot, chopping the ball high in front of the plate, and scooting to first base. He retired with a .341 average, including a .424 mark in 1897 when he hit in 44 straight games—the NL record mark Pete Rose later tied. In 1899, his only home run was an inside-the-park grand slam.

# BILLY WILLIAMS

**OUTFIELDER • ELECTED 1987**

A textbook swing and metronomic reliability—not glitzy heroics or successions of stat titles—made Williams a Hall of Famer. Mired on mostly inept Cubs teams, the six-time All-Star once held the NL record with 1,117 consecutive games played. In 13 straight campaigns, he collected at least 20 homers and 80 RBI. In 1972, Williams was *The Sporting News* Major League Player of the Year and the NL batting champ (.333).

# CARL YASTRZEMSKI

## OUTFIELDER / FIRST BASEMAN ⚾ ELECTED 1989

The great Red Sox left fielder made 18 All-Star teams, won seven Gold Gloves, and landed three batting titles. He is the only player to number 450 home runs among his 3,000 hits in the American League.

How big was Yaz in Boston? By 1968—the year after he won baseball's most recent Triple Crown—he held licensing agreements for clothing, ice cream, milk, muffins, phonograph records, children's books, myriad games, potato chips, mayonnaise, baseball equipment, hot dogs, and even Big Yaz Special Fitness Bread.

# AL SIMMONS

Simmons played 20 years with numerous teams but is best remembered as a star of Connie Mack's great Athletics squads of the 1920s and early 1930s. The hard-playing, hard-living outfielder, who hit .333 in three World Series for them, bested .300 and drove in 100 runs each of the first 11 years of his career.

> **"If I could only have nine players like Simmons…"**
>
> **—Connie Mack, musing on his managerial career**

# RALPH KINER

Kiner won the home run crown in each of his first seven seasons—a feat still unmatched. He slugged 329 long balls from 1946 to 1953, but would hit only 40 more in the rest of his career. He was deprived of bigger numbers because he spent three years as a Navy pilot before starting his career and was debilitated by a bad back in his early 30s. His rate of one homer per every 14.1 at-bats is superior to that of such mashers as Ted Williams, Mickey Mantle, and Jimmie Foxx. Kiner, one of the more popular and generous baseball stars, is in his fourth decade as a Mets TV broadcaster.

# TY COBB

**OUTFIELDER / MANAGER**  **ELECTED 1936**

When a reporter asked Cobb in the late 1950s how well he thought he would hit against modern pitchers, he responded, "Probably only about .290. You have to remember I'm over 70 years old now." He was only half-joking. Conventional wisdom says that the Tigers outfielder was the purest of all hitters. A 12-time batting champ, Cobb finished with a .366 career average—the highest in history. Only Rickey Henderson scored more runs; only Pete Rose collected more hits; and only Sam Crawford legged out more triples.

"The Georgia Peach" was also the most infamously miserable superstar ever. Embittered as a teen by the accidental killing of his father by his mother, Cobb blustered through his career with a tempestuous demeanor and nary a good word to say about anyone but himself.

**"When I began playing the game, baseball was about as gentlemanly as a kick in the crotch."**

—Cobb, justifying his reputation for dirty play

# COOL PAPA BELL

**OUTFIELDER** 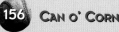 **ELECTED 1974**

Weighing in at a "cool" 140 pounds, James Bell might be the fastest man ever to incinerate a basepath. He was a seven-time Negro League All-Star whom Satchel Paige claimed had the ability to flip a light switch and be in bed before the room went dark. Although the majors didn't integrate until Bell was 43, he was influential in helping other players chip away at the color barrier. In 1946, he sat out games to avoid qualifying for the Negro League batting title so that Monte Irvin could win it and attract the attention of major-league scouts.

# LOU BROCK

## OUTFIELDER ● ELECTED 1985

### Unstoppable Base Thief

- Second all time in career stolen bases (938).
- Led NL eight times.
- Set NL mark with 118 in 1974.
- Holds record with seven in a World Series (twice).
- Shares World Series record for thefts in a game (three) and career (14).

### Underrated Hitter

- Stroked 3,023 hits.
- Ranked among NL top ten in batting average five times.
- Owns highest World Series average (in 75-plus at-bats) in history at .391.

# BABE RUTH

## PITCHER / OUTFIELDER ⚾ ELECTED 1936

If the home run had an "inventor," if there was such a thing as the original sports icon, if a superhero could actually be flesh and blood, Babe Ruth was all those things—and more. Was he the greatest hitter ever? The evidence:

- 12-time home run leader who, when he retired in 1935, had hit 336 more than any other player.

- Career slugging percentage of .690 remains a record by a monstrous 56 points and is 100 points better than all but eight others.

- Retired with 192 batting and pitching records.

- Was the first player ever to hit 30, 40, 50, and 60 home runs in a season.

- In 1920, with 54 homers, broke his own record by 25—and out-homered all but one *team* in baseball, not including his Yankees.

# ROLE REVERSAL

On August 7, 1915, outfielder Sam Rice started on his path to Cooperstown by playing in his first major-league game— but as a relief pitcher. Rice, a tragic figure whose parents, wife, and children had been killed by a tornado three years earlier, went on to rip 2,987 hits but pitch in only eight more games. The right fielder in Rice's mound debut that day was none other than Walter Johnson who, of course, would become a Hall of Fame pitcher.

# PAUL WANER

In 1927, when The Babe was causing such a ruckus by hitting 60 home runs, the overlooked NL MVP with a Ruthian appetite for revelry was Paul Waner. Despite only nine long balls, he raked .380 with 131 RBI. For 14 years, he and his Hall of Fame brother, Lloyd, played in the same Pirates outfield, combining for 5,185 hits. A Brooklyn fan said this about them, as only a Brooklynite could: "Them Waners! It's always the little poison on thoid and the big poison on foist"—thus the origin of their nicknames, "Big Poison" (Paul) and "Little Poison" (Lloyd).

# INEPT TO IMMORTAL

In this Hall of Famer's rookie year, he:

• Was almost involved in an outfield collision in his first game.

• Started his career 0-for-12 at the plate.

• Was picked off second immediately after stealing his first base.

• Had a ball carom off his head in center field for a double.

• Lost an inside-the-park homer because he failed to touch third base.

• Grounded into three double plays in a World Series game.

• Hit the World Series fly ball on which Mickey Mantle suffered the knee injury that would impact his entire career.

Who was this slow-starting superstar?

WILLIE MAYS

"I can't believe **Babe Ruth** was a better player than **Willie Mays.**"

—Sandy Koufax

# ROBERTO CLEMENTE

## OUTFIELDER ✦ ELECTED 1973

Roberto Clemente once said he simply wanted to be remembered "as a ballplayer who gave all he had to give." On New Year's Eve, 1972, the great Pirates right fielder gave his life when his plane crashed while delivering relief supplies to earthquake-devastated Nicaragua. It was an untimely end to a career abundant with baseball and philanthropic triumphs.

## CLEMENTE THE BALLPLAYER

Batted .317 with 240 home runs and exactly 3,000 hits...12-time All-Star...12 consecutive Gold Gloves...1966 NL MVP...Four-time batting titlist...Two-time world champion...MVP of 1971 World Series.

# CLEMENTE THE LEGACY

Inspiration for Roberto Clemente Award, which is given to the player who combines on-field achievement with off-field altruism . . . Namesake of numerous schools, parks, and athletic facilities around the world, many of which benefited from his charity . . . Posthumously awarded the Presidential Medal of Freedom . . . Second baseball player to appear on a postage stamp . . . Right-field wall at PNC Park is 21 feet high in honor of "No. 21."

"He made the word 'superstar' seem inadequate. He had about him a touch of royalty."

—Former baseball commissioner Bowie Kuhn

# DETROIT TIGERS

If you were the Tigers manager, wouldn't you like to present this lineup card to the umpire?

| Catcher | Mickey Cochrane | 1934–1937 |
| Catcher | Mickey Cochrane | 1934–1937 |
| First Base | Hank Greenberg | 1930, 1933–1941, 1945–1946 |
| Second Base | Charlie Gehringer | 1924–1942 |
| Third Base | George Kell | 1946–1952 |
| Shortstop | Hughie Jennings | 1907, 1909, 1912, 1918 |
| Outfield | Ty Cobb | 1905–1926 |
| Outfield | Al Kaline | 1953–1974 |
| Outfield | Goose Goslin | 1934–1937 |
| Pitcher | Jim Bunning | 1955–1963 |

# WHEN BAD THINGS HAPPEN TO GOOD PLAYERS...

Hall of Famers comprise seven of the top ten on the list of post-1900 outfielders with the most errors—headed by Ty Cobb's 271.

On July 28, 1971, Brooks Robinson, perhaps the greatest third baseman who ever lived, committed three errors in the same inning.

▶ Heinie Manush got tossed from a 1933 World Series game when he pulled back and snapped an umpire's bow tie that was attached with an elastic band.

Babe Ruth is the only player to be caught stealing to end a World Series (1926).

# DUKE SNIDER

Even in Terry Cashman's song "Talkin' Baseball"—aka "Willie, Mickey & The Duke"—Snider seemed to be the third wheel of New York center fielders in the 1950s. However, the "Silver Fox" out-homered them both (and everyone else) with 326 in the decade. He also was integral to the franchise's first two world championships, clubbing 11 long ones in 36 Fall Classic tilts.

> "When they tore down Ebbets Field, they tore down a little piece of me."

**—Snider**

## REFLECTIONS ON REGGIE

"The only thing Reggie can do better on the field than me is talk."

—Rod Carew

"Reggie's really a good guy. He'd give you the shirt off his back. Of course, he'd call a press conference to announce it."

—Catfish Hunter

"The best thing about being a Yankee is getting to watch Reggie play every day. The worst thing? Getting to watch Reggie play every day."

—Graig Nettles

# LARRY DOBY

Less than three months after Jackie Robinson blazed the trail with the Dodgers in 1947, Larry Doby integrated the American League with the Indians. By 1948, he was a .300 hitter on a World Series champ. In 1949 he commenced a seven-year run as an All-Star. For a 1954 team that won a then-record 111 games, the skilled center fielder was the AL home run (32) and RBI (126) leader. In 1978, he became MLB's second African-American manager, helming a White Sox team whose roster included a catcher named Larry Doby Johnson.

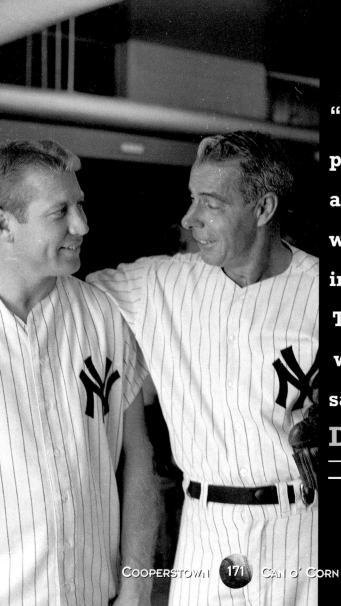

"**Heroes** are people who are all good with no bad in them. That's the way I always saw Joe DiMaggio."

—**Mickey Mantle**

# TAKES ONE TO KNOW ONE

In 1953, the Cleveland Indians dispatched a scout to see a kid tearing it up in American Legion ball in Fargo, North Dakota. "Have your father phone me as soon as you get home," instructed the impressed birddog. Soon, for a $5,000 bonus, the 18-year-old—by the name of Roger Maris—was under contract. The scout was future Hall of Fame first baseman Hank Greenberg, whose 58 home runs in 1938 had matched the most ever by an American Leaguer other than Babe Ruth—until Maris whacked 61 for the Yankees eight years later.

Roger Maris

Hank Greenberg

# HANK GREENBERG

## FIRST BASEMAN / OUTFIELDER ⚾ ELECTED 1956

"I shook my fist at Hitler every time I hit a home run."

—Greenberg

### Timeline

**1911:** Born in New York City to Romanian Jewish parents.

**1929:** Accepts basketball scholarship to New York University after failing baseball tryouts with Senators and Giants.

**1930:** Signs with Detroit Tigers.

**1933:** Bashes .301 as a Tigers rookie.

**1934:** Leads Tigers to pennant but sits out playoff game on Yom Kippur.

**1935:** Wins AL MVP Award as Detroit captures its first World Series.

**1937:** Drives in 183 runs, one shy of AL record.

**1938:** Slugs 58 homers, tying record for righty hitters.

**1940:** Wins second MVP Award, leading Tigers to pennant.

**1941:** Joins military and misses most of five seasons.

1. Ted Williams          .344
2. Babe Ruth             .342
3. Jimmie Foxx           .325
4. Hank Aaron            .305
5. Mel Ott               .304

# JESSE BURKETT

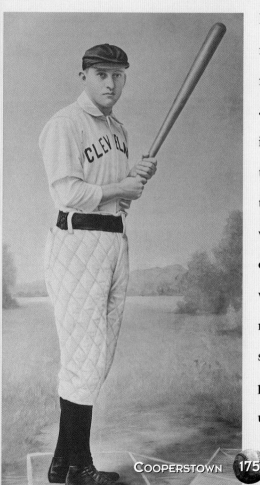

Reports on how many pitching victories Burkett once recorded in a minor-league season range as high as 39, but it was as a combative batter in the bigs that he achieved immortality. On one hand, he could hit like the devil: a .342 lifetime average, with a high of .423 in 1895. On the other, he was an outfielder from hell who made nearly 400 errors. Nicknamed "Crab" for his irascible disposition, Burkett once was dragged by police from an argument with an umpire, then fined for inciting a riot.

# Hugh Duffy

The highest single-season batting average in baseball history belongs to Hugh Duffy, a pocket-size center fielder who swatted .440 for the 1894 Boston Beaneaters. He hit safely in 107 of his 124 games that year and even led the National League with 18 home runs. Duffy, also a brilliant flychaser, reached .300 11 times and 100 RBI on eight occasions. Later, as a septuagenarian Red Sox scout and coach, he was a tutor to the young Ted Williams.

# WILLIE STARGELL

**OUTFIELDER / FIRST BASEMAN** \ **ELECTED 1988**

## STARGELL THE PLAYER

The Pirates captured two World Series in Stargell's 21 years with the team, including one in 1979, when a 39-year-old "Pops" became the first player to win the league, LCS, and Fall Classic MVP Award. He is the team's all-time leader in homers and RBI.

## STARGELL THE MAN

When Willie was in the minors, a white man with a gun approached him on the street and threatened to kill him if he played that night. Stargell played—and went on to become an ambassador of the game, establishing a foundation to fight sickle cell anemia and winning many community service awards.

"He's got power enough to hit home runs in any park, including Yellowstone."

—Sparky Anderson

# TED WILLIAMS

**OUTFIELDER** ⚜ **ELECTED 1966**

Ted Williams may have been the most intense, fastidious, selective, combative— and best— batsmith in history. It was said that he was able to detect a fraction of an ounce incongruity in the weight of a bat and that he could read the label of a spinning record. A mighty presence of a man, Williams could be confrontational, profane, and arrogant, though also charitable, charismatic, and engaging. As accomplished as he was between the lines, he also became an expert naval aviator, a champion fly fisher, and an author.

"The Splendid Splinter": Won six batting titles...was the last man to hit .400 (1941)...poked 521 homers with 1,839 RBI...holds the all-time on-base percentage record (.482)... ranks second to Babe Ruth in slugging (.634)...won two MVP Awards and two Triple Crowns.

"All I want out of life is that when I walk down the street, people will say 'There goes the greatest hitter who ever lived.'"

—Williams

# WHEN BAD THINGS HAPPEN TO GOOD PLAYERS...

◄ **Kid Nichols** allowed 12 runs in the first inning of a game on September 21, 1897, something that was never approached until August 13, 2006, when Kansas City's Luke Hudson allowed 11 in the first.

The all-time strikeout leaders in both leagues are Hall of Famers: Reggie Jackson (2,597 in the AL) and Willie Stargell (1,936 in the NL).

Eddie Collins was barred from playing his senior year at Columbia University because he was found to have played a year of pro ball under an assumed name, "Eddie Sullivan."

▶ **Robin Roberts** allowed more home runs (505) than any other pitcher in history.

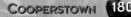

**OUTFIELDER** ◊ **ELECTED 1961**

**CATCHER / OUTFIELDER / INFIELDER** ◊ **ELECTED 1945**

"Sliding" Billy Hamilton, who stood all of 5'6", wreaked havoc on 19th-century opponents with equal parts alacrity and audacity. His crossed home plate 192 times in a season, stole seven bases in a game, and averaged 1.06 runs scored per contest in his career—all singular achievements.

Almost concurrently, fans were screeching, "Slide, Kelly, Slide!" every time the daring—and outrageous—Michael "King" Kelly reached base. Kelly stories abound: the time as player/manager he raced out of the dugout yelling "Kelly now catching" and nabbed a foul pop…and the time in fading daylight he ran from the outfield apparently cradling the game-ending catch in his glove, only to admit later the ball had gone over his head for a home run.

# FRANK ROBINSON

## OUTFIELDER / MANAGER ⚬ ELECTED 1983

"Robby" has made a profound impact on virtually every crevice of the game—as a winner of nearly every conceivable playing award and statistical title, a two-time World Series champ for the Orioles, a pioneering manager and activist, and a front-office executive/consultant for Major League Baseball.

## Frank's Firsts

- First to win MVP Award in each league

- First to club 200 home runs in each league

- First Oriole to win the Triple Crown (1966)

- First Oriole to have his number (20) retired

- First African-American to manage a major-league team (1975 Indians)

# WHO IN THE HALL...?

1) WAS THE FIRST PLAYER TO HAVE HIS SIGNATURE REPRODUCED ON A LOUISVILLE SLUGGER BAT?

2) IS THE ONLY PLAYER TO KNOCK IN 1,000 RUNS WITH HOMERS AND 1,000 MORE IN OTHER WAYS?

3) WAS THE FIRST PLAYER TO START AT THREE DIFFERENT POSITIONS IN THE SAME WORLD SERIES?

4) IS THE ONLY INDUCTEE OFFICIALLY LISTED AS A DESIGNATED HITTER?

5) PLAYED FOR THE SO-CALLED "WORST TEAM OF ALL TIME" — THE 1962 METS?

**1)** Honus Wagner, in 1905 **2)** Hank Aaron **3)** Willie McCovey (1B, RF, LF) **4)** Paul Molitor **5)** Richie Ashburn

# DAVE WINFIELD

**OUTFIELDER ⚾ ELECTED 2001**

## Timeline

**1951:** Born on same day Bobby Thomson hits "the shot heard 'round the world."

**1972:** Plays on Big Ten championship basketball team for University of Minnesota.

**1973:** Becomes only man drafted by four leagues (NBA, ABA, NFL, MLB's Padres).

**1981:** Joins Yankees as the game's highest-paid player (10 years, $23 million).

**1983:** Accidentally kills a seagull with a thrown ball.

**1987:** Awarded seventh Gold Glove.

**1988:** Makes last of 12 All-Star teams.

**1992:** Wins World Series with Blue Jays.

**1995:** Retires as third player (Aaron, Mays) with 3,000 hits, 450 homers, and 200 steals.

# Cooperstown Quiz

**1)** To what team was Jackie Robinson (who retired instead of reporting) traded in 1956?

**2)** Who was the only member of the inaugural Hall of Fame class to receive more votes than Babe Ruth?

**3)** Who is the only Hall of Famer to have played for the Devil Rays?

**4)** For which team was Joe DiMaggio a coach?

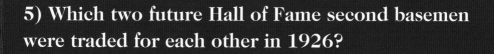

**5)** Which two future Hall of Fame second basemen were traded for each other in 1926?

**1)** New York Giants **2)** Ty Cobb **3)** Wade Boggs **4)** The Oakland A's, in 1968 and 1969 **5)** Rogers Hornsby and Frankie Frisch

 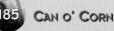

# CHAPTER FOUR
# TOEING THE SLAB

## "You don't save a pitcher for tomorrow. Tomorrow it might rain."

—Leo Durocher

Manager Durocher of the Cubs waits for his relief pitcher to come to the mound.

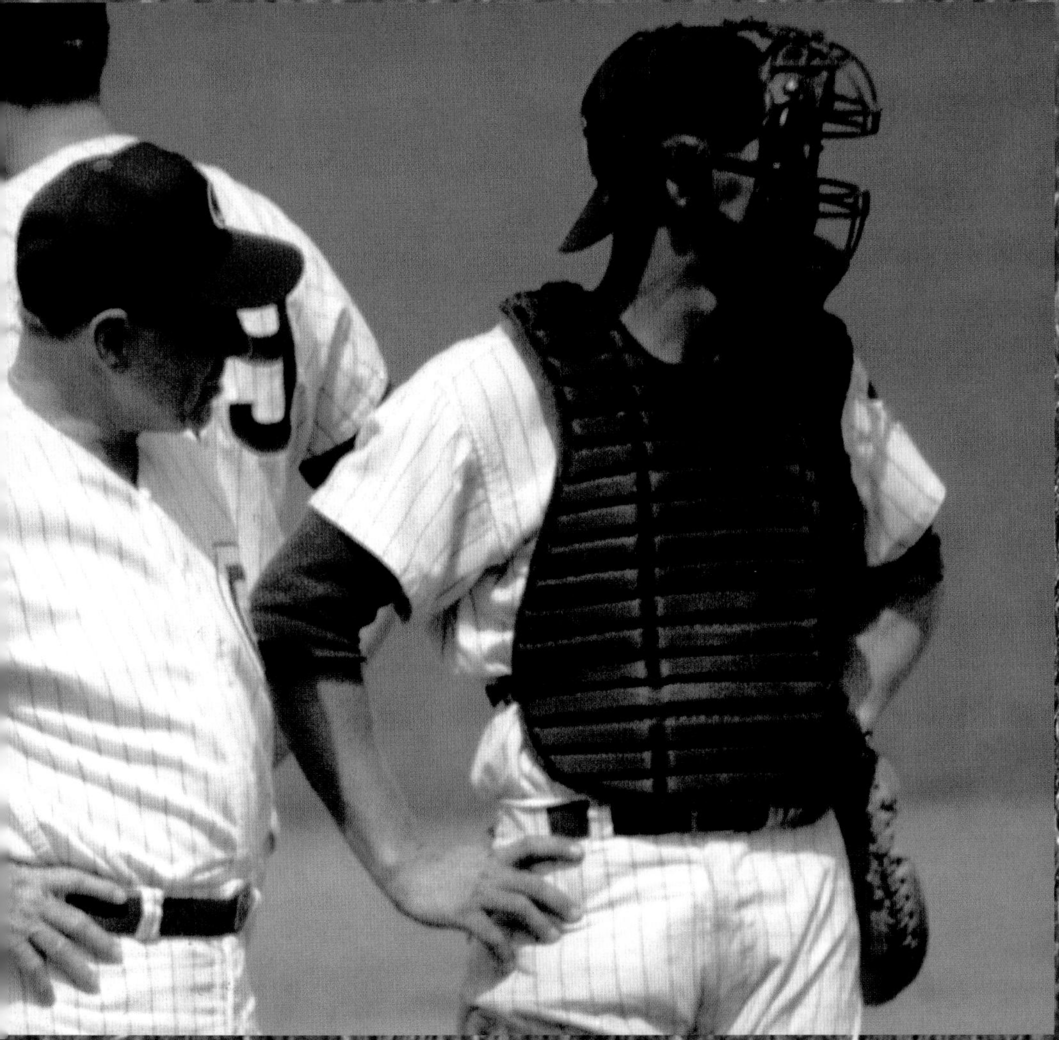

# NOLAN RYAN

**PITCHER ✢ ELECTED 1999**

Two of the first four batters Nolan Ryan faced in his major-league debut were Hall of Famers Eddie Mathews and Hank Aaron. He retired them both. And 22,575 batters later—one of every four of them a strikeout victim—Ryan concluded a career with a slew of pitching achievements that may never be matched.

- All-time strikeout leader with 5,714—more than 1,000 ahead of the next best, Roger Clemens—4,604 (2006).

- Seven no-hitters—three more than anyone else.

- 11-time league strikeout leader.

- Most whiffs in a season (383 in 1973).

- Twice as many 300-strikeout seasons (six) as any other right-hander.

- Fanned 21 Hall of Famers and 47 MVPs.

- Only pitcher to strike out Roger Maris, Mark McGwire, Sammy Sosa, and Barry Bonds.

- Oldest pitcher to win an All-Star Game, pitch a no-hitter, and have a 300-strikeout season.

- Played more seasons (27) than any other player.

"Ryan is the only guy who puts **fear into me**— not because he can get you out, but because he can **kill you.**"

—Reggie Jackson

# WHITEY FORD

PITCHER ● ELECTED 1974

No left-hander in history owns a better winning percentage than Whitey Ford, who went 236–106 (.690) for the 1950–67 Yankees. And he was always at his best in October. Starting 22 World Series, games during which he compiled a 2.71 ERA, the "Chairman of the Board" collected six rings and set records for wins (10) and consecutive scoreless innings (33).

> **"If you had one game to win and your life depended on it, you'd want him to pitch it."**
>
> **—Casey Stengel on Ford**

# Dizzy Dean

## PITCHER ⚜ ELECTED 1953

Dizzy Dean was a clown out of the womb, a dropout at age 10, a soldier at 16, an MVP at 24, and a has-been with a bum shoulder at 28. The NL's last 30-game winner (for the world-champion 1934 "Gas House Gang"), Dean continued to make his mark on the game for two more decades as an announcer, where he described how "runners slud into third" and mediocre pitchers had "nothin' on the ball 'cept a cover." The St. Louis Board of Education once mounted an effort to have him taken off the air because of his man-gled English. (They failed.)

"When ol' Diz was out there pitching, it was more than just another ballgame. It was a **regular three-ring circus,** and everybody was wide awake and enjoying being alive."

—Teammate Pepper Martin

# Catfish Hunter

**PITCHER ⚾ ELECTED 1987**

As a boy growing up in rural North Carolina, Jim Hunter used money he earned selling frogs to local restaurants to buy his first baseball. More than 20 years later, his seminal free agency challenge earned him the largest contract ($3.5 million) in baseball history to that point. "Catfish" (nicknamed by slick Oakland owner Charlie Finley for marketing purposes) pitched the A's and Yankees to multiple World Series titles. In 1968, he hurled a perfect game, and from 1971 to 1976, he averaged 21 wins.

# WHO IN THE HALL...?

**1)** IS ALSO A MEMBER OF THE MEXICAN AND CUBAN HALLS OF FAME?

**2)** HAD A STATISTICAL TITLE NAMED AFTER HIM WHILE HE WAS STILL ACTIVE?

**3)** WAS THE FIRST BASEBALL PLAYER TO BE FEATURED ON A POSTAGE STAMP?

**4)** ONCE LED HIS LEAGUE IN HOME RUNS WITHOUT HITTING ANY OF THEM OVER THE FENCE?

**5)** HAD FOUR BROTHERS WHO ALSO PLAYED IN THE MAJORS?

**1)** Martin Dihigo **2)** The Lou Brock Award, to the majors' top base thief **3)** Jackie Robinson **4)** Ty Cobb with 9 in 1909 **5)** Ed Delahanty (Frank, Jim, Joe, and Tom also played ball)

# Martin Dihigo

### PITCHER ⚾ ELECTED 1977

"**The greatest player I ever saw** was a black man. He's in the Hall of Fame, although not a lot of people have heard of him. His name is Martin Dihigo. I played with him in Santo Domingo in winter ball of 1943. He was the only guy I ever saw who **could play all nine positions, run and was a switch-hitter.** I thought I was havin' a pretty good year myself down there and they were walkin' him to get to me."

—Johnny Mize

# RUBE WADDELL

With a name like Waddell, it's not surprising the Rube was an "odd duck." He regularly missed games, choosing instead more favored activities such as fishing, chasing fire trucks, wrestling alligators, shooting marbles, and frequenting local honky-tonks. Once, to keep his sleep-deprived roommate from quitting the team, the Athletics wrote into Rube's contract that he was no longer allowed to eat animal crackers in bed. Managers forgave Waddell's eccentricities because, by 1902, he was the game's best left-hander. His 349 Ks in 1904 were an MLB record for 69 years.

# WALTER JOHNSON

## PITCHER  ELECTED 1936

The game's first true power pitcher, Johnson's near-100-mph fastballs made him a phenomenon in his day. In fact, his career strikeout record of 3,509 lasted 56 years—longer than Babe Ruth's mark of 714 home runs.

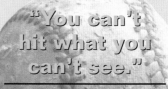

"You can't hit what you can't see."

—**John Daley of the St. Louis Browns, after facing Walter Johnson in 1912**

"The Big Train" (called "Plain Walt" before he got famous) won three pitching triple crowns and two AL MVP Awards in a career that spanned 1907–1927. His 417 wins are an American League record, and his 110 shutouts are 20 more than anyone else has spun in either league.

## No Support

- Won 60 percent of his decisions for teams that otherwise won 46 percent of their games.

- Lost 27 games by a score of 1–0.

- Won 38 games by a score of 1–0.

- 65 of his losses came when Senators were shut out.

- Lost 20 games despite a 1.90 ERA in 1916.

# NEW YORK/SAN FRANCISCO GIANTS

**If you were the Giants manager, wouldn't you like to present this lineup card to the umpire?**

| | | |
|---|---|---|
| Catcher | Buck Ewing | 1883–1889, 1891–1892 |
| First Base | Willie McCovey | 1959–1973, 1977–1980 |
| Second Base | Frankie Frisch | 1919–1926 |
| Third Base | Freddie Lindstrom | 1924–1932 |
| Shortstop | Dave Bancroft | 1920–1923, 1930 |
| Outfield | Willie Mays | 1951–1952, 1954–1972 |
| Outfield | Mel Ott | 1926–1947 |
| Outfield | Ross Youngs | 1917–1926 |
| Pitcher | Christy Mathewson | 1900–1916 |

# GAYLORD PERRY

## PITCHER ⚜ ELECTED 1991

Perry won 314 games in 22 seasons for eight teams. He was the first pitcher to win the Cy Young Award in each league, doing so for the 1972 Indians (24–16, 1.92) and the 1978 Padres (21–6, 2.73).

His great moments included a 15-strikeout game in 1966 (a year in which he won 20 of his first 22 decisions); a 1968 no-hitter to outlast Bob Gibson, 1–0; and the rare career achievement of beating every team in both leagues.

Perry's inclusion in the Hall was controversial because of widespread contention that he often doctored the ball with foreign substances. He admitted as much in his auto-biography, *Me and the Spitter.*

# MAGIC NUMBERS

**2** Times daily Rollie Fingers had to wax his handlebar moustache to keep it curly at the ends.

**7** Consecutive complete games won in the World Series by Bob Gibson.

**243** Games played as a teenager by Robin Yount (ML record).

**756** Home runs Hank Aaron would have hit had he not had one nullified for stepping out of the batter's box.

**25,000** Dollars that a silver dollar, thrown by Walter Johnson 300 feet across the Rappahannock River, sold for in the 1980s.

# BOB GIBSON

## PITCHER ✦ ELECTED 1981

Gibson's hitter-humbling combo of a blazing fastball and agitated intensity produced more than 250 wins and 3,000 strikeouts, a 7–2 record and 1.89 ERA in three World Series (he was MVP in two of them), and a pair of Cy Young Awards.

## SINGULAR SEASON

Statistically, Gibson's great 1968 season is often regarded as the best ever by a starting pitcher.

- 1.12 ERA is baseball's best since 1913.

- 13 shutouts are most since 1916.

- Only time in history a pitcher threw 300 innings and allowed fewer than 200 hits.

- Set World Series record with 17 strikeouts in Game 1.

# GROVER CLEVELAND ALEXANDER

**PITCHER ⚾ ELECTED 1938**

There is little evidence that Grover Cleveland "Pete" Alexander was a happy man anywhere but on the mound, where he made hitters miserable for 20 years. He was quiet, afflicted with epileptic fits and alcoholism, and traumatized and partially deafened from World War I combat. He once lapsed into a two-day coma after being hit by a ball. At times, however, "Old Pete" was as good as there ever was. His 373 wins match Christy Mathewson's for the most in National League history.

 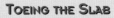

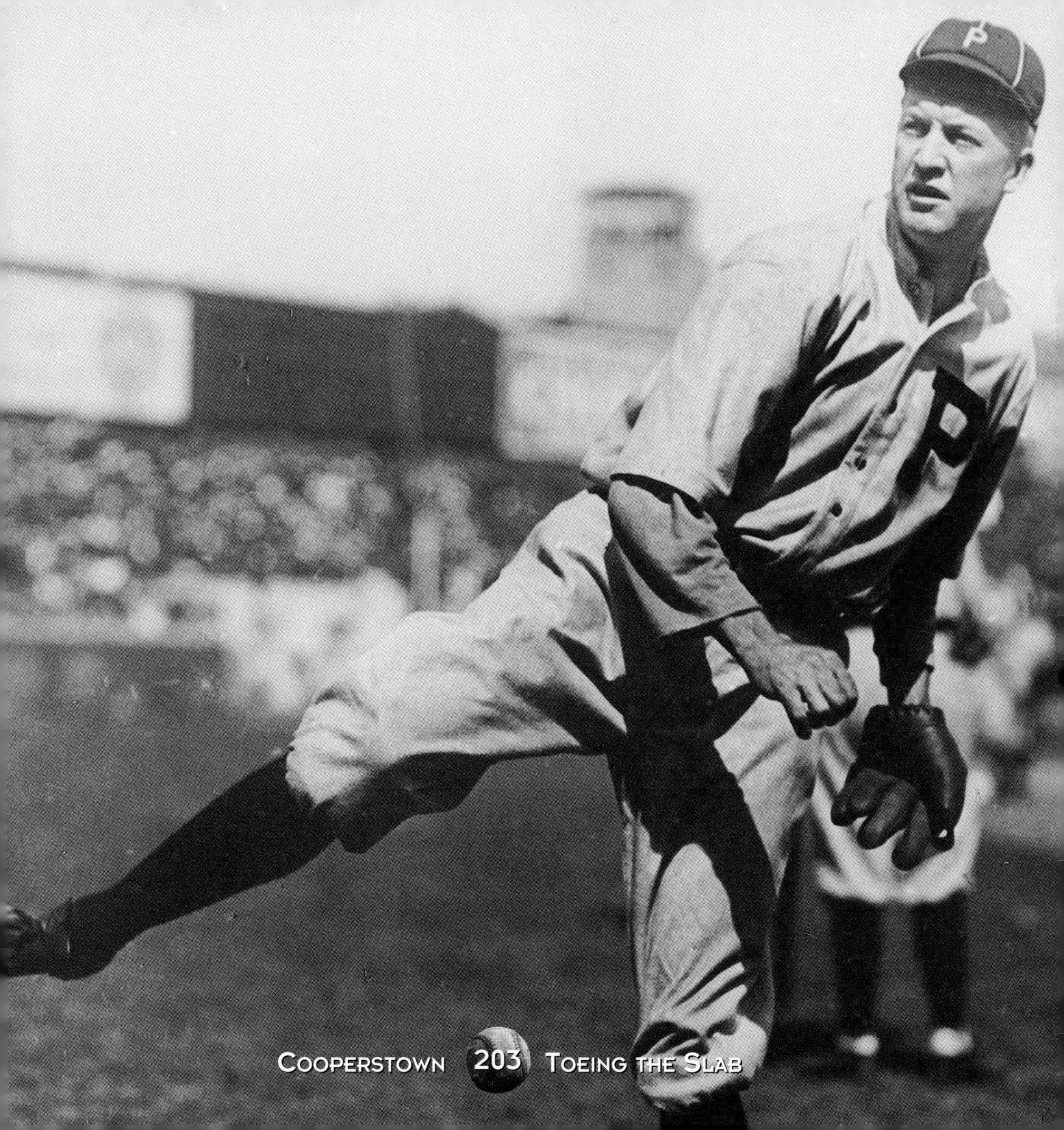

# BOB FELLER

## WAY TO GO, YOUNG FELLER

**Age 16:** Agrees to terms for $1 but is too young to sign contract himself.

**Age 17:** Strikes out 15 in his first start for Indians and 17 three weeks later.

**Age 19:** Sets still-standing record of 208 walks in a season but throws his first of 12 one-hitters and is the first to fan 18 in a game.

**Age 20:** Youngest pitcher to win 20 games in a season (and remains so in AL).

**Age 21:** Fires Opening Day no-hitter and wins AL pitching triple crown.

**Age 23:** Joins Navy; serves for nearly four years.

**Age 27:** With 348, comes within one of MLB single-season strikeout record.

**Age 32:** Ties record with third no-hitter.

**Age 43:** Becomes first pitcher since Walter Johnson elected to the Hall on first ballot.

# WHEN BAD THINGS HAPPEN TO GOOD PLAYERS...

Warren Spahn surrendered a home run to 75-year-old Hall of Famer Luke Appling in an old-timer's game.

Moments after George Brett ripped the 3,000th hit of his career, he was picked off first base.

The last hit Bob Gibson ever gave up was a pinch-hit grand slam.

The Giants originally purchased Christy Mathewson from a minor-league team, but when he lost his first three decisions they demanded their money back.

The only two pitchers in the modern era to walk 200 men in a season are Nolan Ryan ▶ (twice) and Bob Feller.

**PITCHER ⚾ ELECTED 1947**

Curiously, Grove was underappreciated—perhaps because his combustible personality made him the star everyone loved to hate. He had a fastball with as much giddyup as any southpaw's in history. Lefty led the AL in SOs in each of his first seven campaigns. He is the lone pitcher to top the AL in ERA four straight seasons (1929–1932) and the only man in either league to do it nine times in all.

"He could throw a lamb chop past a wolf."

—Sportswriter Arthur "Bugs" Baer on Grove's fastball

# A PAIGE OUT OF HISTORY

Satchel Paige's actual age—listed at 59 when he threw three scoreless innings for the 1965 Athletics—will forever be a mystery, as it was even to himself. It seems his mother Lula etched the birthdates of her 13 children into the family Bible.

Unfortunately, while Satchel's father was reading it under a chinaberry tree one day, this page blew out of his hands and was eaten by the family goat.

|  | W–L | SHO | Hits/9 IP | BB/9 IP | SO/9 IP | ERA |
|---|---|---|---|---|---|---|
| 1955–60 | 36–40 | 5 | 7.58 | 5.27 | 8.88 | 4.10 |
| 1961–66 | 129–47 | 35 | 6.45 | 2.27 | 9.44 | 2.19 |
| World Series | 4–3 | 2 | 5.68 | 1.74 | 9.63 | 0.95 |

**"A foul ball was a
moral victory."**

**—Fellow Hall of Famer
Don Sutton on his teammate**

# SANDY KOUFAX

## PITCHER ● ELECTED 1972

For six seasons, Koufax was a kid with an extraordinary fastball and ordinary results. For the next six, he may have been the best there ever was. From 1961 through 1966, of the possible 18 NL ERA, wins, and strikeouts titles, he won 12. En route to three World Series titles with the Dodgers and a like number of Cy Young Awards, he authored four no-hitters (one a perfect game) and set a record for strikeouts per nine innings (9.28) that endured until Nolan Ryan showed up. An arthritic elbow forced Sandy to retire at age 30.

# TOM SEAVER

## PITCHER ● ELECTED 1992

His rights acquired in a lottery when the word "Mets" was picked out of a hat, Seaver put that once-hapless franchise on the map. He was a three-time Cy Young Award winner and the poster boy for the 1969 "Miracle Mets," for whom he went 25–7. "Tom Terrific," who is the only pitcher to fan 200 or more batters in nine straight seasons, once estimated that he was able to put 24 of every 25 pitches exactly where he wanted. In 1992, he was ushered into the Hall with a record percentage of the vote.

# CARL HUBBELL

## PITCHER ⚜ ELECTED 1947

By the time he retired, Hubbell's left arm was a pretzeled appendage, twisted inward nearly 180 degrees after throwing thousands of screwballs. He practically invented the pitch, yet as a Tigers farmhand, he was prevented from using it by manager Ty Cobb. Sold to the Giants, he had only one losing season out of 16.

- **First pitcher to be a two-time MVP**

- **Set lefty record with 45⅓ straight scoreless innings, 1933**

- **Fanned five future Hall of Famers in succession in the 1934 All-Star Game**

- **Holds record with 24 consecutive wins, 1936–1937**

# CHIEF BENDER

PITCHER ❧ ELECTED 1953

He signed his name "Charley," but "Chief" Bender (whose mother was Chippewa) was the first Native American elected to the Hall of Fame. Here's why:

- Won 212 games, including a 193–102 record for the 1903–1914 Philadelphia A's.

- Compiled a 2.46 ERA and allowed only 40 home runs in 3,017 innings.

- Entered a 1906 game in the sixth inning, played left field, and hit two inside-the-park homers.

- Pitched a no-hitter and a shutout back-to-back in 1910.

 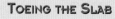

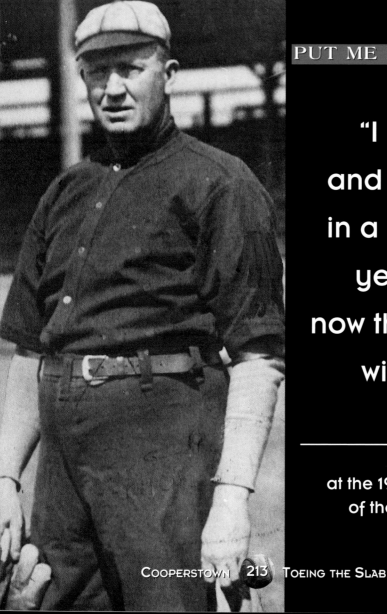

"I do hope and root that in a hundred years from now the game will still be greater."

—Cy Young
at the 1939 dedication
of the Hall of Fame

# WARREN SPAHN

## PITCHER ❧ ELECTED 1973

Spahn was 25 years old before his career got out of the "cup of coffee" stage, yet he threw more innings (5,243⅔) and won more games (363) than any left-hander in history. Featuring a high leg kick, numerous variations on his pitches, and an unmatched acumen for his craft, he equaled Christy Mathewson's record for 20-win seasons with 13. Spahn won the Cy Young Award with the 1957 Braves and fired two no-hitters.

> **"Hitting is timing. Pitching is upsetting timing."**
>
> —**Spahn**

# FERGIE JENKINS

## PITCHER ⚜ ELECTED 1991

- First man in history to pitch at least 4,500 innings and strike out more than three men for every one he walked.

- 20-game winner for six straight Cubs teams from 1967 to 1972, despite losing five 1–0 games in 1968.

- Won the 1971 Cy Young Award.

- Was the first Canadian elected to the Hall of Fame.

# CHRISTY MATHEWSON

## PITCHER  ELECTED 1936

There were a lot of screwballs in the rough-edged game of baseball at the turn of the 20th century. Christy Mathewson—ironically a generous, educated, refined gentleman who wouldn't pitch on Sundays—simply

threw one. It happened to be the best one ever. For the 1900–1916 New York Giants, he won nearly 400 games while fashioning ERAs below 2.30 in 11 seasons. At the conclusion of his playing days, Mathewson joined the Army briefly and then, at 45, died of tuberculosis contracted from being gassed in a military training exercise.

- Owns eighth-lowest ERA of all time (2.13).

- Threw two no-hitters.

- Led NL in strikeouts five times.

- Compiled walk-free streaks of 47 and 68 innings (the latter a record for 49 years) in 1913.

"Mathewson was the greatest pitcher who ever lived. He had knowledge, judgment, perfect control and form. It was wonderful to watch him pitch when he wasn't pitching against *you*."

—Connie Mack

# Don Drysdale

**PITCHER ⚾ ELECTED 1984**

When Drysdale retired in 1969, he had hit more batters with pitches (154) than anyone in the National League since 1900. The intimidation factor (magnified by his 6′6″ stature), as well as a crackling fastball and steely will, generated three strikeout crowns and the 1962 Cy Young Award, when he went 25–9. Drysdale's most celebrated feat is his 58 consecutive scoreless innings (including six straight shutouts) in 1968, a record that stood for 20 years. The Dodgers rode him and Sandy Koufax to three world championships.

# BROOKLYN/LOS ANGELES DODGERS

**If you were the Dodgers manager, wouldn't you like to present this lineup card to the umpire?**

| | | |
|---|---|---|
| Catcher | Roy Campanella | 1948–1957 |
| First Base | Eddie Murray | 1989–1991, 1997 |
| Second Base | Jackie Robinson | 1947–1956 |
| Third Base | Freddie Lindstrom | 1936 |
| Shortstop | Pee Wee Reese | 1940–1942, 1946–1958 |
| Outfield | Duke Snider | 1947–1962 |
| Outfield | Joe Medwick | 1940–1943, 1946 |
| Outfield | Paul Waner | 1941, 1943–1944 |
| Pitcher | Sandy Koufax | 1955–1966 |

# Cooperstown Quiz

1) Who is the only pitcher to have fired an Opening Day no-hitter?

2) Which pitcher caught the first Opening Day pitch from a sitting president?

3) Which "M and M" immortals share a record by playing in 24 consecutive All-Star Games?

4) Who won the Triple Crown in 1966 yet never led his league in any of those categories at any other time in his career?

5) When Whitey Ford pitched 33⅓ consecutive scoreless World Series innings, whose 43-year-old record of 29⅔ did he break?

6) Whose real name was Aloysius Szymanski?

7) Who are the only full brothers in the Hall of Fame?

8) Who captured more league strikeout crowns than any other pitcher?

Lloyd Waner 8) Walter Johnson (12)
and Willie Mays 4) Frank Robinson 5) Babe Ruth 6) Al Simmons 7) Paul and
1) Bob Feller 2) Walter Johnson, from William Taft in 1910 3) Stan Musial

# MORDECAI BROWN

## PITCHER  ELECTED 1949

The last two times the Cubs won the World Series, it was thanks to Mordecai Brown. Making the ball dance with a right hand mutilated in a farm accident, "Three Finger" fired shutouts in both of his Fall Classic starts in 1907 and 1908 and collected another win in relief. In fact, his five-year span of greatness might have been baseball's best pitching performance ever. Check out these historical hot streaks:

| | PERIOD | ERA |
|---|---|---|
| Mordecai Brown | 1906–10 | 1.42 |
| Ed Walsh | 1906–10 | 1.50 |
| Walter Johnson | 1910–16 | 1.56 |
| Pete Alexander | 1915–20 | 1.64 |
| Addie Joss | 1904–09 | 1.67 |

# ED WALSH

## PITCHER ❦ ELECTED 1946

- All-time lowest career ERA (1.82).

- Went 18–20 in 1910 despite a 1.27 ERA.

- Majors' last 40-game winner, when he pitched 464 innings for the 1908 White Sox.

> **"I think the ball disintegrated on the way to the plate and the catcher put it back together again. I swear, when it went past the plate, it was just the spit that went by."**
>
> **—Sam Crawford on Walsh's spitball**

# SATCHEL PAIGE

## PITCHER • ELECTED 1971

"Age," said Satchel Paige, "is a question of mind over matter. If you don't mind, it doesn't matter." And apparently it didn't to the greatest Negro League pitcher of all time. A combination of hard data, his own estimates, and some ambiguous stats put his career numbers at something like 2,500 games pitched, 2,000 wins, 300

shutouts, and 50 no-hitters amassed at hundreds of locations—wherever they would let a black man pitch. They finally let him pitch in the majors at the age of 42 (or thereabouts), and Paige made a couple of All-Star teams for the St. Louis Browns. In 1965, at age 59, Satch mustered three scoreless innings for the Kansas City Athletics.

## SATCH'S RULES FOR STAYING YOUNG

1. Avoid fried meats, which angry up the blood.

2. If your stomach disputes you, lie down and pacify it with cool thoughts.

3. Keep the juices flowing by jangling around gently as you move.

4. Go very lightly on the vices, such as carrying on in society. The social ramble ain't restful.

5. Avoid running at all times.

6. Don't look back. Something might be gaining on you.

# BRUCE SUTTER

## PITCHER ● ELECTED 2006

Arm surgery at age 20 was a blessing in disguise for Sutter. Forced to come up with a new wrinkle, he developed a split-finger fastball—now a staple of many, but rare in the 1970s. That pitch made him the first great National League closer. Sutter won the 1979 Cy Young Award with the Cubs, and his 45 saves for the 1984 Cardinals stood as a league record for seven years. He retired as the third 300-save man.

# "Winning isn't everything. Wanting to win is."

**—Catfish Hunter, in his 1987 induction speech**

*Hunter (left) holds his HOF plaque with Peter Ueberroth, commissioner of Major League Baseball (1984–1989).*

# DON SUTTON

## PITCHER ● ELECTED 1998

**The Early Years:** Sutton began his career as a strike-out pitcher, whiffing 209 (most by an NL rookie in 66 years) and topping 200 Ks in five of his first eight seasons.

**Mid-Period Sutton:** As he became more of a "pitcher," success followed. He helped his Dodgers to three pennants from 1974 to 1978, posting nine straight winning records.

**The Golden Years:** Don pitched until he was 43, only twice in 23 seasons failing to win 10 games. He is still the Dodgers' all-time leader in wins (233), strikeouts (2,696), and shutouts (52).

# Jim Bunning

## PITCHER \\ ELECTED 1996

## Skill on the Hill

- First pitcher since Cy Young to win 100 games and strike out 1,000 batters in each league.

- Pitched a no-hitter for the 1958 Tigers and a perfect game for the 1964 Phillies.

- When he retired in 1971, was second to Walter Johnson in career strikeouts (2,855).

Bunning is currently serving his second term as a U.S. senator from Kentucky.

# ROLLIE FINGERS

While playing with matches when he was eight years old, Rollie accidentally set fire to a neighbor's house. He spent his young adulthood putting fires out. The all-time saves leader with 341 when he retired, the mustachioed right-hander slammed doors for three Oakland A's championship teams in the '70s. In 33⅓ World Series innings, Fingers compiled a 1.35 ERA with two wins and six saves. In 1981, he became the first reliever to win the MVP and Cy Young Award in the same year.

# THE SULTAN OF SWAP

## Babe at the Plate

Plate Appearances............10,616

Home Runs ...........................714

HR Rate .......................1 per 14.9

## Babe on the Mound

Batters Faced.....................5,006

Home Runs Allowed ...............10

HR Rate ....................1 per 500.6

"All us
Youngs
could throw.
I used to kill
squirrels
with a stone
when I was
a kid, and
my grand-
dad once
killed a
turkey
buzzard on
the fly with
a rock."

—Young

# CY YOUNG

## PITCHER ✶ ELECTED 1937

Named "Denton True" after the soldier who saved his father's life in the Civil War, and nick-named "Cyclone" when his pitches shattered a wooden backstop, Young clearly holds more unbreak-able records than any pitcher. Among them: 511 wins, 7,354⅔ innings pitched, 749 com-plete games, 24 consecutive no-hit innings, and fifteen 20-win campaigns. There can be no greater testament to his great-ness than having the annual award for each league's best pitcher named in his honor.

"Let liquor severely alone, fight shy of cigarettes, and be moderate in indulgence of tobacco, coffee, and tea... A man who is not willing to work from dewy morn until weary eve should not think about becoming a pitcher."

—Two of Young's "Six Rules for Pitching Success," 1908

## EXTRA BASES

# THE MICK FOR A SONG

Mickey Mantle's salary as a rookie in 1951 was $5,000. He never made more than $100,000 in a year, even taking a $10,000 cut in 1960 following a season in which he hit "only" 31 homers. In 1968, three-quarters of his pay was deferred—without interest—over the next three years. In his entire career, The Mick earned $1,123,000. In 2006, the *average* yearly salary for a major-leaguer was $2,866,544.

# MAGIC NUMBERS

**29** Ty Cobb's age when he recorded his 2,000th hit as the only man to do it before turning 30.

**4,072** Days in between George Brett's first cycle (single, double, triple, and homer in the same game) and his second — a record.

**52** Games played by Willie McCovey in 1959, when he was the unanimous NL Rookie of the Year.

**12** Inside-the-park home runs (a record) by Sam Crawford in 1901.

**84** Years between National League perfect games, spun by John Ward (1880) and Jim Bunning (1964).

# JACK CHESBRO

Spitballing "Happy Jack" Chesbro is the answer to these trivia questions:

Who, in 1903, was the starting pitcher in the New York Yankees' (then the Highlanders) first game?

Who, in 1904, started (51) and won (41) more games in a season than any pitcher in modern history?

Who is the only known player to be discovered while playing for the team of a mental hospital?

# STEVE CARLTON

The debate over who is the best southpaw of all time is quintessential baseball. None was better than Sandy Koufax—but he was great only for a relatively short time. Warren Spahn has more wins than any other, Randy Johnson more strikeouts, and Whitey Ford and Lefty Grove the best winning percentages. Steve Carlton, however, leads lefties in Cy Young Awards (4), ranks second in whiffs (4,136) and wins (329), and is third in shutouts (55). He won a World Series with the Cardinals, made ten All-Star teams, set an NL record with six one-hitters, and once struck out 19 in a game.

# Joe McGinnity

As a young minor leaguer, Joe "Iron Man" McGinnity once pitched all 21 innings of a game. In the majors, he pitched and won both ends of a doubleheader three times in a month and topped 400 innings in back-to-back years. Returning to the minors at age 44, he did the doubleheader thing yet again, and—at 52!—pitched a 268-inning season. But here's the surprising part: McGinnity got his nickname from working in his father-in-law's foundry.

# EDDIE PLANK

## PITCHER ✦ ELECTED 1946

Plank's tics, twitches, wiggles, fidgets, and blasted procrastinations made him an impatient hitter's nightmare in the early 20th century. His cat-and-mouse act helped him win the third-most games (326) ever by a left-hander but was a drain on the attendance at Philadelphia's Shibe Park, as fans would invariably miss their trains home due to the interminable duration of Plank's starts.

"[Plank] was not the fastest, not the trickiest, and not the possessor of the most stuff. He was just the greatest."

**—Eddie Collins**

# The Hall's Hardest Throwers

**NOLAN RYAN** was timed by the *Guinness Book of World Records* at 100.9 miles per hour.

In 1914, **WALTER JOHNSON** was "timed" at 99.7 mph when one of his pitches was measured against a speeding motorcycle.

Johnson himself submitted, "No man alive can throw a baseball harder than **JOE WOOD**."

**BOB FELLER** claimed to have once been clocked at 107.9 mph.

Former Commissioner Ford Frick insisted, "He [**LEFTY GROVE**] was the fastest pitcher who ever lived."

"My fastball looks like a change of pace alongside that little pistol bullet ol' Satchel [Paige] shoots up to the plate."

—Dizzy Dean

# JIM PALMER

Palmer made a huge splash in 1966 when, at age 20, he became the youngest pitcher to throw a shutout in the World Series—to beat Sandy Koufax, no less. After overcoming career-threatening injuries the next two years, he carved out a magnificent 19-year run with the Orioles. A winner of 268 games, he was the first AL pitcher to land three Cy Young Awards.

## Lowest ERAs Since 1960
### (3,000+ Games)

| | |
|---|---|
| 1. Jim Palmer | 2.856 |
| 2. Tom Seaver | 2.862 |
| 3. Juan Marichal | 2.890 |

# WHO IN THE HALL...?

1) BECAME THE FIRST FORMER MAJOR LEAGUE NON-PITCHER TO PLAY PROFESSIONALLY IN JAPAN?

2) COMPRISED TWO-NINTHS OF BASEBALL'S FIRST ALL-BLACK STARTING LINEUP ON SEPTEMBER 1, 1971?

3) ARE THE ONLY THREE PITCHERS INDUCTED WITH A LOSING RECORD IN THE MAJOR LEAGUES?

4) BROKE THE ELBOW OF A HALL OF FAMER BY HITTING HIM WITH A PITCH, AND LATER HAD HIS OWN LEG BROKEN BY A LINER OFF THE BAT OF ANOTHER HALL OF FAMER?

5) WERE TEAMMATES AT LOCKE HIGH SCHOOL IN LOS ANGELES?

1) Larry Doby, with Chunichi in 1962 2) Roberto Clemente and Willie Stargell of the Pirates 3) Satchel Paige, Rollie Fingers, and Bruce Sutter 4) Bob Gibson (broke Duke Snider's elbow; Roberto Clemente broke Gibson's leg) 5) Eddie Murray and Ozzie Smith

# DENNIS ECKERSLEY

## PITCHER ● ELECTED 2004

"The Eck" was a good enough starting pitcher to win more than 150 games, throw a no-hitter, and make two All-Star teams. It was as a reliever, however, that he not only earned his Hall of Fame credentials but also became the prototype of the modern closer. Ironically, Dennis is generally credited with inventing the term "walk-off home run."

- Fifth all-time in saves, with 390.

- Only pitcher with at least 150 wins and 200 saves.

- In 1990, allowed only five earned runs and 45 base-runners in $73\frac{1}{3}$ innings.

- 1992 AL Cy Young and MVP Award winner.

# JUAN MARICHAL

## PITCHER ● ELECTED 1983

If one assumes that Marichal threw five different pitches out of five different motions, then batters had 25 insurmountable problems. Most days, they had no chance. Juan—who once was thrown in jail for five days after losing an important game for the Dominican Air Force—was MLB's winningest pitcher from 1963 through 1969. In his major-league debut for the Giants, he retired the first 19 Phillies and tossed a one-hitter. "The Dominican Dandy" retired with 243 wins and a dandy 2.89 ERA.

# CHAPTER FIVE

# OUT OF THE YARD

## "The players make the manager; it's never the other way."

—Hall of Fame manager
Sparky Anderson

Anderson sits alone in the Detroit Tigers dugout during the 1988 season.

# CASEY STENGEL

## MANAGER ✹ ELECTED 1966

No more entertaining character—and perhaps no more adroit manager—than Stengel ever stepped between the white lines. "The Old Perfessor" skippered the 1949–60 Yankees to ten pennants and seven World Series titles, only once winning fewer than 92 games. An unaffected clown, Casey delivered incoherent homilies, once doffed his cap to liberate a sparrow, danced jigs on the dugout steps, dozed on the bench—and collected the 11th-most managerial wins (1,905) in history.

# AN ABRIDGED DICTIONARY OF STENGELESE

**"Butcher boy"**
— a chopped ground ball

**"He could squeeze your earbrows off."**
— a strong player

**"Plumber"**
— a good fielder

**"Road apple"**
— a poor player

**"The youth of America"**
— rookies

**"Whiskey slick"**
— a womanizer

**"Worm killer"**
— a low pitch

# KENESAW MOUNTAIN LANDIS

## COMMISSIONER ✠ ELECTED 1944

Baseball's first commissioner, the commanding, flamboyant, often despotic and stubborn Landis measured a mere 5´6˝ and 135 pounds, but he threw his weight around. In his tenure from 1920 to 1944 he

- consolidated virtually absolute control of the game.

- presided over the cleanup of the Black Sox scandal and other incidences of corruption, expelling numerous players.

- suspended Babe Ruth for barnstorming and Ty Cobb for fighting.

- declared such future Hall of Famers as Heinie Manush and Bob Feller free agents when they were minor leaguers.

- advocated for and officially opened the Hall of Fame.

# Bill Veeck, Jr.

**EXECUTIVE**  **ELECTED 1991**

As the innovative, maverick, over-the-top owner of the Indians, Browns, and White Sox from 1946 to 1980, Veeck left these imprints on the game:

- Integrated the American League

- Planted the ivy at Wrigley Field

- Sent 3′7″ Eddie Gaedel to the plate (he drew a walk)

- Introduced the exploding scoreboard

- Allowed fans to manage a 1951 game by holding up "yes" or "no" placards

- Popularized premium giveaways

- Brought the first world title in 28 years to Cleveland

- Built the first pennant-winner in 40 years for 1959 White Sox

- Set attendance records with almost every team he led

# THEY MADE THE RIGHT CALLS

The best umpires are those who are never noticed—at least until they retire. Eight of them have been elected to the Hall of Fame.

The first, in 1953, were Tom Connolly (who umped the first game ever played at Yankee Stadium as well as the premier at Fenway Park) and Bill Klem. Many say Klem was the greatest of all—so good that for 16 years, he was prohibited from working in the field simply because he was so proficient at calling balls and strikes.

*Tom Connolly*

• Jocko Conlan was a White Sox outfielder when he umpired his first major-league game in 1935. Because he was a licensed boxing ref, he was drafted off the bench to call a Chicago–St. Louis contest when the regular ump fell ill.

• Nestor Chylak, who used his eyes to make a living, had nearly been blinded at the Battle of the Bulge in World War II.

• Cal Hubbard, also a member of the Pro Football and College Football Halls of Fame, is the only inductee to three major sports halls.

*Bill Klem*

# YOU ARE WHAT YOU WEAR

Based on the jersey numbers displayed on Hall of Fame plaques, some trivia:

**Lowest: 1 (Richie Ashburn, Earle Combs, Bobby Doerr, Rabbit Maranville, Pee Wee Reese, Ozzie Smith)**

**Highest: 65 (Bill McKechnie)**

**Highest by a Player: 53 (Don Drysdale)**

**Most Popular: 4 (Luke Appling, Joe Cronin, Lou Gehrig, Goose Goslin, Ralph Kiner, Ernie Lombardi, Paul Molitor, Duke Snider, Earl Weaver, Hack Wilson)**

**Least Popular: 12, 13, 25, 28, 40, 46, 47, 48, 50–52, 54–64, 66 and up (none)**

# Tommy Lasorda

## MANAGER  ELECTED 1997

Lasorda was born eight days before Babe Ruth hit his 60th home run in 1927. He later became one of baseball's great ambassadors and characters. A former Dodgers pitcher, scout, and minor-league skipper who claims to "bleed Dodger blue," he managed the team from 1976 to 1996, winning four NL pennants and two World Series. Tommy's cheerleading style, profane (often comical) tirades, and gregarious glad-handing have made him a beloved figure. He became a Dodgers executive, managed a U.S. team to its first Olympic gold medal in baseball, and currently travels the country making inspirational speeches and supporting charities.

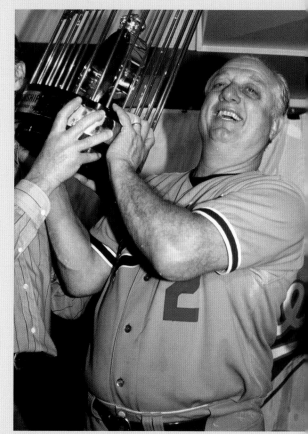

# "She Loved Baseball"

So reads the gravestone of Effa Manley, co-owner of the storied Newark Eagles (which developed Larry Doby, Monte Irvin, and Don Newcombe) from 1936 to 1948. In an era when blacks were barred from the major leagues and women were socially disempowered, Manley turned her Negro Leagues ballclub into a champion on the field and an instrument of civil rights. Treasurer of the local NAACP chapter, she even staged an "Anti-Lynching Day" at her ballpark in 1939.

As an activist owner, Manley's advocacy helped secure fair contracts for her players, even for those who jumped to the majors. To ensure them a wage during the off-season, she and husband Abe sponsored a team on which they could play in Puerto Rico in the winter. There is even a yarn

*Leniel Hooker, Max Manning, Jim Brown, and Raleigh "Biz" Mackey (left to right) of the Newark Eagles (June 1939)*

that tells of her giving players signs during the game—by crossing and uncrossing her legs.

In 2006, a quarter-century after her death as the last surviving owner of a black baseball franchise, a special committee elected Manley as the first woman to dignify the Hall of Fame.

# CONNIE MACK

## MANAGER ⚾ ELECTED 1937

At the inaugural Hall of Fame induction ceremony, Honus Wagner recounted how he used to walk or hitchhike 14 miles just to see Connie Mack play ball. But it was as a street clothes-wearing manager that "The Tall Tactician" forged his unique legacy. For 50 years, he helmed the Philadelphia Athletics (a team he owned), winning nine pennants and five World Series. His 3,731 wins are nearly 1,000 more than anyone else can claim.

"Well, you can't win them all."

—Mack on his 1916 A's, who went 36–117

# JOE MCCARTHY

## MANAGER 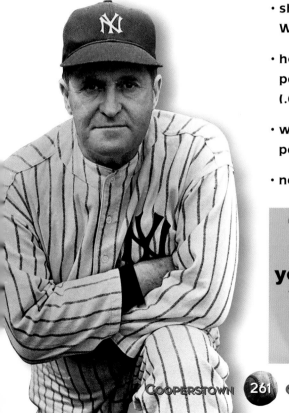 ELECTED 1957

The numbers indicate that McCarthy—who managed the Cubs for five years, the Yankees for 16, and the Red Sox for three—was the most successful field general who ever lived. He

- shares the record for the most World Series titles (seven).

- holds the records for winning percentage in the regular season (.615) and World Series (.698).

- was the first manager to win pennants in each league.

- never had a losing season.

> ## "You can't manage yourself; how can you manage others?"
>
> —McCarthy to Babe Ruth, who wanted to succeed him as Yankees manager

"I have seen many Negro players who should be in the major leagues. There is no room in baseball for discrimination. It is our national pastime and a game for all."

—Lou Gehrig

"Someday I was going to have to meet my maker and if he asked me why I didn't let the boy play and I said it was because he was black, that might not be a satisfactory answer."

—Baseball commissioner Happy Chandler, speaking of Jackie Robinson

# THE ROSTER

Through 2008, there were 286 members of the National Baseball Hall of Fame. They include

**Major Leaguers: 199**

**Negro Leaguers: 35**

**Executives/Pioneers: 26**

**Managers: 19**

**Umpires: 8**

**Elected by Baseball Writers Association: 104**

**Elected by Veterans Committee: 153**

**Elected by Negro Leagues Committees: 27**

**Living/Deceased: 65/221**

# ONLY THE HALL WAS WHITE

"I hope someday Satchel Paige and Josh Gibson will be voted into the Hall of Fame as symbols of the great Negro players who are not here."

With those words at his 1966 induction speech, Ted Williams catalyzed an interminably overdue movement to open the doors of the Hall to players and luminaries of the Negro Leagues. Within six years, they were opened. Satch, however, wasn't impressed with the new wing.

*The Negro League Entrance Exhibit at the Baseball Hall of Fame in Cooperstown*

"The one change," he said late in his life, "is that baseball has turned Paige from a second-class citizen into a second-class immortal."

Until 2006, the roster of greats from the pre-integration era numbered a paltry 18. That total swelled instantly to 35 through an election by a special committee, as an array of Negro Leaguers and pre-Negro Leagues players and executives were inducted as part of the largest Hall of Fame class in history.

*Oscar Charleston, Rap Dixon, Josh Gibson, Judy Johnson, and Jud Wilson (left to right) of the Pittsburgh Crawfords*

# THE CLASS OF 2006

The 2006 induction class was historic and unique—18 strong, and all but one (Bruce Sutter) was elected by the Negro Leagues/Pre-Negro Leagues Committee. The group was a who's who of the greatest players and pioneering executives of "black baseball." Delivering the keynote speech was 94-year-old Buck O'Neill—a former Negro Leagues player/manager, the first black coach in the majors, and a beloved emissary of the game—whose own exclusion from the list of inductees was widely considered a travesty. Still, baseball immortal Monte Irvin said, "What happened today was something that I thought would never happen."

**RAY BROWN**
PITCHER

**WILLARD BROWN**
CENTER FIELDER

**ANDY COOPER**
PITCHER

**FRANK GRANT**
SECOND BASEMAN

**PETE HILL**
CENTER FIELDER

**BIZ MACKEY**
CATCHER

**EFFA MANLEY**
PIONEER/EXECUTIVE

**JOSÉ MÉNDEZ**
PITCHER

**ALEX POMPEZ**
PIONEER/EXECUTIVE

**CUM POSEY**
EXECUTIVE

**LOUIS SANTOP**
CATCHER

**MULE SUTTLES**
FIRST BASEMAN

**BEN TAYLOR**
FIRST BASEMAN

**CRISTÓBAL TORRIENTE**
CENTER FIELDER

**SOL WHITE**
PIONEER/EXECUTIVE

**J. L. WILKINSON**
PIONEER/EXECUTIVE

**JUD WILSON**
THIRD BASEMAN

# WHO IN THE HALL...?

**1) PITCHED NO-HITTERS DURING THE TERMS OF THREE DIFFERENT U.S. PRESIDENTS?**

**2) WAS THE ONLY PITCHER TO WIN 20 GAMES AND BAT .400 IN THE SAME SEASON?**

**3) ARE THE ONLY TWO PLAYERS IN HISTORY TO STEAL A BASE IN FOUR DIFFERENT DECADES?**

**4) GRACED THE COVER OF THE FIRST EDITION OF SPORTS ILLUSTRATED?**

**1)** Cy Young **2)** Walter Johnson (20–7, .433 in 1925) **3)** Ted Williams and Rickey Henderson **4)** Eddie Mathews, on August 16, 1954

# GEORGE WRIGHT

## SHORTSTOP ⚬ ELECTED 1937

Wright is regarded as the finest baseball player of the Civil War era. The brother of fellow Hall of Famer Harry Wright (himself a pioneer of the sport and a legendary manager), George was a brilliant shortstop and batsmith for the Cincinnati Red Stockings, the first openly all-professional team. They were rarely beaten, in large part due to Wright's batting averages that sometimes ranged into the .600s and power that generated roughly one home run per game. In the 1870s, Wright starred for six league-title-winning teams in Boston.

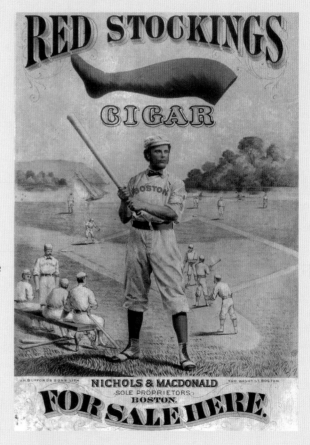

 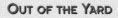

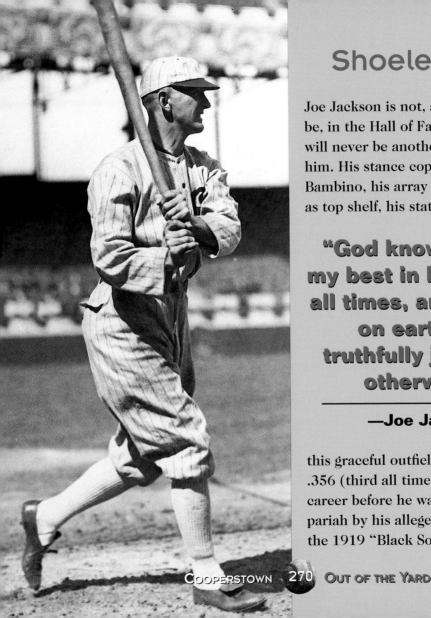

# Shoeless Joe

Joe Jackson is not, and may never be, in the Hall of Fame. But there will never be another player like him. His stance copied by The Bambino, his array of tools regarded as top shelf, his stats unassailable,

**"God knows I gave my best in baseball at all times, and no man on earth can truthfully judge me otherwise."**

**—Joe Jackson**

this graceful outfielder batted .356 (third all time) in a 13-year career before he was made a baseball pariah by his alleged involvement in the 1919 "Black Sox" scandal.

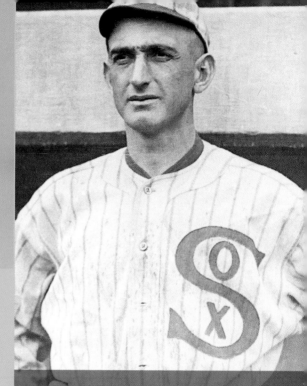

> "I copied Jackson's style because I thought he was the greatest hitter I had ever seen.... He's the guy who made me a hitter."
>
> —Babe Ruth

Jackson, nicknamed "Shoeless Joe" after playing a minor-league game in his stocking feet, was banished from the game along with seven team-mates following accusations of accepting payola to throw the 1919 World Series. He has since emerged as the most sympathetic character of the group—an illiterate, awkward, and impressionable country bumpkin who, after all, batted .375 and hit the Series' only homer in the loss to the Reds.

> "Say it ain't so, Joe! Say it ain't so!"
>
> —A young boy to Jackson as he exited the courthouse where he was acquitted of charges

# KINERISMS

**Once a slaughterous slugger, Ralph Kiner is now a long-esteemed baseball announcer—even if he sometimes slaughters the language. Among his deadly lines:**

- "All of his saves have come during relief appearances."

- "It's a nice day for baseball if it doesn't rain."

- "He's going to be out of action the rest of his career."

- "If Casey Stengel were alive today, he'd be spinning in his grave."

- "The Hall of Fame ceremonies are on the 31st and 32nd of July."

# WALTER ALSTON

For the duration of 23 one-year contracts, Walter "Smokey" Alston managed the Dodgers with a mysterious, impassive efficiency that frustrated the quote-hungry media but infused his players with a ladle of stability and a *soupçon* of fear. The formula bore more than 2,000 wins, four World Series titles, and seven pennants between 1954 and 1976.

"Look at misfortune the same way you look at success: Don't panic. Do your best and forget the consequences."

**—Alston**

# BASEBALL AS AMERICA

If you can't get to Cooperstown, perhaps Cooperstown can come to you.

The Hall of Fame has taken its show on the road with a themed exhibition of baseball memories. Since 2002, the "Baseball As America" display has appeared at museums around the nation.

Billed as "the first major exhibition to examine the relationship between baseball and American culture," "Baseball As America" displays approximately 500 artifacts, including the "Doubleday Ball" from the mythic first game and the most valuable baseball card in the world, the T206 Honus Wagner.

# BRANCH RICKEY

**EXECUTIVE** ⚾ **ELECTED 1967**

Branch Rickey was probably the most genuinely revolutionary force in the history of baseball. His list of contributions and innovations over his 42 years as a general manager is stunning—headlined, of course, by his orchestration of the Jackie Robinson situation, imploding the game's color barrier in the mid-1940s. Some others: He invented the concept of the farm system, created uniform training and instructional techniques for his teams, and was among the authors of modern statistical analysis.

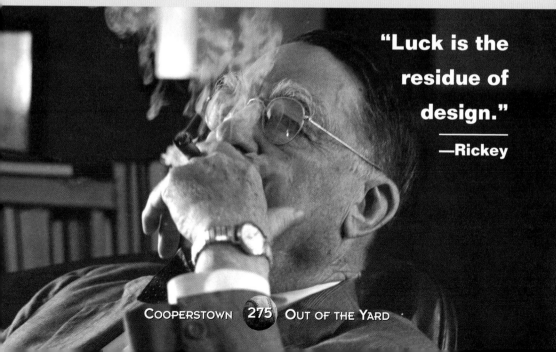

"Luck is the residue of design."

—Rickey

# IMMORTAL WORDS AND VOICES

Visitors to Cooperstown can peruse the "Scribes & Mikemen" exhibit in the Library of the National Baseball Hall of Fame. It is there that the game's greatest writers and broadcasters are immortalized.

At the annual Hall of Fame Induction Ceremony, one from each discipline is recognized. To a writer goes the J. G. Taylor Spink Award, named for its first recipient in 1962, the longtime publisher and editor of *The Sporting News.*

In 1978, the Ford C. Frick Award was established to honor the giants of baseball broadcasting, starting with Red Barber and Mel Allen. Barber was the first baseball radio man in New York, calling Dodgers, then Yankees, games. In 1939, "The Old Redhead" was at the mike for the sport's first telecast, a Dodgers–Reds matchup. Allen, perhaps the most recognizable voice in sports broadcasting history, intoned Yankees games from 1939 through 1964 and hosted the classic *This Week in Baseball* TV show for 19 years.

*J. G. Taylor Spink*

## J. G. Taylor Spink Award

Bob Addie
Bob Broeg
Heywood C. Broun
Warren Brown
Si Burick
John Carmichael
Murray Chass
Gordon
  Cobbledick
Ritter Collett
Phil Collier
Dan Daniel
John Drebinger
Charles Dryden
Joseph Durso
Joe Falls
Charley Feeney
Hugh Fullerton
Peter Gammons
Frank Graham
Tommy Holmes
Jerome Holtzman
Bob Hunter

James Isaminger
Harold Kaese
Ray Kelly
John F. Kieran
Leonard Koppett
Sam Lacy
Jack Lang
Ring Lardner
Earl Lawson
Hal Lebovitz
Allen Lewis
Fred Lieb
Hal McCoy
Joe McGuff
Tom Meany
Sid Mercer
Edgar Munzel
Tim Murnane
Jim Murray
Ross Newhan
Shirley Povich
Joe Reichler
Grantland Rice

Milton Richman
Tracy Ringolsby
Damon Runyon
Bus Saidt
Harry G. Salsinger
Ken Smith

Red Smith
Wendell Smith
J. G. Taylor Spink
Bob Stevens
J. Roy Stockton
Dick Young

## Ford C. Frick Award

Mel Allen
Red Barber
Marty Brennaman
Jack Brickhouse
Jack Buck
Buck Canel
Harry Caray
Herb Carneal
Jerry Coleman
Jimmy Dudley
Bob Elson
Gene Elston
Joe Garagiola
Curt Gowdy
Milo Hamilton
Ernie Harwell

Russ Hodges
Jaime Jarrin
Harry Kalas
Arch McDonald
Bob Murphy
Lindsey Nelson
Bob Prince
Rafael "Felo"
  Ramírez
By Saam
Vin Scully
Lon Simmons
Chuck Thompson
Bob Uecker
Bob Wolff

## PUT ME IN, COACH

**"I guess that after surviving the Battle of the Bulge, confronting Billy Martin in front of 50,000 fans doesn't seem that scary."**

—Bob Chylak, at the induction of his late father, umpire Nestor Chylak

**"There's two kind of managers. One that ain't very smart. He gets bad players, loses games, and gets fired. Then there was somebody like me that was a genius. I got good players, stayed out of the way, let 'em win a lot, and then just hung around for 26 years."**

—Sparky Anderson, 2000 induction speech

# SPARKY ANDERSON

## MANAGER ⚾ ELECTED 2000

Hyperbolic—and often just plain hyper—Anderson was a loquacious leader who won two Manager of the Year Awards in each league.

Says the always self-deprecating Anderson:

> **"Me carrying a briefcase is like a hog wearing earrings."**
>
> **—Anderson**

| | | W–L | Win % | Pennants | WS Wins |
|---|---|---|---|---|---|
| Reds, | 1970–78 | 863-586 | .596 | 4 | 2 |
| Tigers, | 1979–95 | 1,331-1,248 | .516 | 1 | 1 |
| Total | | 2,194-1,834 | .545 | 5 | 3 |

# JOHN MCGRAW

**MANAGER ⚾ ELECTED 1937**

McGraw owns the most-overlooked .334 career batting average in history—unnoticed because, while there have been better third base-men, there may never have been a better manager. With a combination of competitive bluster and scientific brilliance, McGraw skippered the Giants from 1902 to 1932, winning ten pennants and three World Series along the way.

Dubbed "Little Napoleon" for his doctrinaire micromanagement, he may be second to Connie Mack in all-time victories, but his .586 winning percentage is 100 points higher.

> "There has been only one manager, and his name is John McGraw."
>
> —Connie Mack

# THE BOY AND "THE MAN"

On May 2, 1954, an eight-year-old Nate Colbert was in the stands in St. Louis to watch Stan Musial lace five home runs in a double-header against the Giants. Eighteen years later, Colbert, playing for the Padres, would become only the second player to achieve that feat—and it hasn't been done since.

# Field of Dreams

Even a flabby, frustrated, 50-something fan can feel like a Hall of Famer for a week by participating in the institution's fantasy camp. Open to only 48 entrants, the event is held each October in Cooperstown, where several Hall of Famers serve as camp managers and former players act as coaches, offering playing tips and participating in the games, drills, and frivolities.

Campers are lodged at a luxury hotel, get to play on hallowed Doubleday Field, are treated to a private candlelight dinner in the Hall of Fame Gallery, and are given a private, behind-the-scenes tour of the Museum. Come armed with golf clubs, starry eyes, and a stocked checkbook—participants paid a cool $7,995 for the 2006 event.

*At the fantasy camp, there are both fielding (left) and batting (right) instructions.*

# Cooperstown Quiz

1) Who is the Hall's only pitcher never to have started a game?

2) What is Ozzie Smith's real first name?

3) Who was the first manager to win a World Series in each league?

4) Which future Hall of Famer was the Dodgers manager when another immortal, Tommy Lasorda, made his major-league debut for them?

5) Which Hall of Famer was born Cornelius Alexander McGillicuddy?

1) Bruce Sutter 2) Osborne 3) Sparky Anderson 4) Walter Alston
5) Connie Mack

# EARL WEAVER

## MANAGER  ELECTED 1996

Weaver's credo was "pitching, defense, and the three-run homer." That philosophy (another way of saying he dug the long ball), along with a razor-sharp strategic mind and a prickly personality that commanded deference, made him the greatest of Orioles managers. His .583 winning percentage (ninth all time) includes four pennants and the 1970 World Series crown. Beyond that, Weaver is regarded as a world-class umpire-baiter. He took belligerence to an art form, pioneering the technique of turning one's cap backwards to get closer to an arbiter's face, feigning heart attacks, absconding with bases, and excavating dirt.

He was ejected nearly 100 times, including three times from both games of a doubleheader.

# PETE ROSE

Few baseball issues send fans scurrying to the opposite sides of the room faster than the debate over whether Pete Rose should be in the Hall of Fame. For the **"YEAS"**: Rose is the all-time hits leader with 4,256, a 17-time All-Star, and the personification of the way the game should be played—with joy, tenacity, and unremitting hustle. For the **"NAYS"**: Commissioner Bart Giamatti concluded the three-time batting champ made large and frequent bets on baseball games, even on the Reds while managing them. As such, Rose was permanently barred from organized baseball—and thus, from Cooperstown.

> "I'D WALK THROUGH HELL IN A GASOLINE SUIT TO PLAY BASEBALL."
>
> —ROSE

**The player's record, playing ability, integrity, sportsmanship, character, and contributions to the team(s) on which the player played shall determine the voting.**

—Paraphrased rules for Election to the National Baseball Hall of Fame by Members of the Baseball Writers' Association of America, Section 5

> "He's the best thing to happen to the game since, well, the game."
>
> —Hall of Fame manager Sparky Anderson

## HALL OF FAME FOLLIES

# WHEN BAD THINGS HAPPEN TO GOOD PLAYERS...

Nolan Ryan holds the record for most grand slams allowed (ten).

Cy Young surrendered hits to the last seven batters he faced in his career.

A couple of legendary Dodgers managers did not fare so well as players. Tommy Lasorda ▶ uncorked three wild pitches in the only inning of his first start, and Walter Alston struck out in his only major-league at-bat.

In 1910, Connie Mack traded Shoeless Joe Jackson (eventual career batting average .356) to Cleveland for Bris Lord, who would hit .256 for his career.

In a 1907 game, Washington stole a record 13 bases off Yankees (then known as the Highlanders) catcher Branch Rickey.

# ALEXANDER CARTWRIGHT

**PIONEER**  **ELECTED 1938**

Cartwright—also known as "The Father of Modern Baseball"—did not invent the game. And contrary to what's written on his Hall of Fame plaque, it's unlikely that his early organization of the game included the basics, such as 90 feet between bases, nine men on a team, and nine innings in a game. However, the chirpy New Yorker certainly was instrumental in the sport's genesis as organizer of the mid-19th-century Knickerbockers, whose early games inspired the evolution of modern baseball as we know it.

# A WEEKEND IN JULY

Ground zero of the National Baseball Hall of Fame experience is Cooperstown on the last weekend of July: the exciting, evocative, emotional Induction Weekend. Festivities include signature-seeking from the dozens of fans who are in attendance, a minor-league ballgame, interactive events, roundtable discussions, book signings, numerous other special programs, and, of course, the induction itself on Sunday.

Admission to the ceremony itself is free, but accommodations can be scarcer than a Babe Ruth autograph, so plan your pilgrimage far in advance.

*Baseball fans wait for the start of the 2006 Baseball Hall of Fame Induction Ceremony on July 30 (larger photo). Later that day, Bruce Sutter gave his acceptance speech at the Clark Sports Center (smaller photo).*

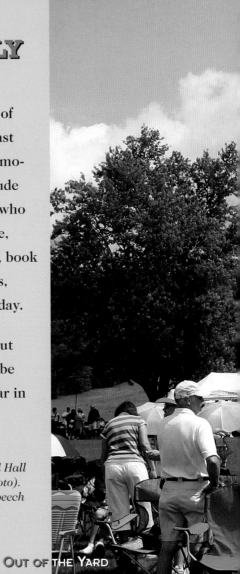

"Had I known
I would have
been up here one
day, I sure would
have saved all
my rookie
baseball cards."

—Dave Winfield, 2001

DAVID MARK WINFIELD
SAN DIEGO, N.L., 1973-1980, NEW YORK, A.L., 1981-1990

# LEO DUROCHER

As polarizing as he was successful, the brassy "Leo the Lip" managed the Dodgers, Giants, Cubs, and Astros to 2,008 wins over 24 seasons—but rarely without controversy. Though terminally embroiled in battles with players, umpires, management, fans, and the media, he won three pennants and (with the 1954 Giants) one World Series. As a player, Durocher was an All-Star shortstop for the Cardinals and Dodgers.

"Show me a **good loser** in professional sports, and I'll show you **an idiot.** Show me a sportsman, and I'll show you a player I'm looking to trade."

—Durocher

# WHO IN THE HALL...?

1) GOT THE ONLY HIT OFF 59-YEAR-OLD SATCHEL PAIGE IN HIS THREE-INNING PITCHING APPEARANCE IN 1965?

2) IS THE ONLY GRANDFATHER EVER TO HIT A MAJOR-LEAGUE HOME RUN?

3) HIT HIS FIRST HOME RUN INSIDE THE PARK AND THE REMAINING 510 OF HIS CAREER OVER THE WALL?

4) WAS A PITCHER IN ONLY THREE OF HIS 1,399 GAMES IN THE 1920S AND THREW COMPLETE-GAME VICTORIES IN HIS ONLY TWO OUTINGS OF THE 1930S?

1) Carl Yastrzemski 2) Stan Musial, at age 42, a few hours after the birth of his grandson 3) Mel Ott 4) Babe Ruth

# RECORD REPRIEVE

Don Drysdale's 58⅔ consecutive scoreless innings in 1968 broke Walter Johnson's record of 55⅔ and stood for 20 years until Orel Hershiser went ⅓ of an inning better. But one of baseball's rarest plays kept Drysdale's streak intact, and one of baseball's weakest hitters ended it. With the streak at 44, Drysdale plunked the Giants' Dick Dietz with the bases loaded. The umpire, however, ruled that Dietz did not try to avoid the pitch and ordered him back in the box. Drysdale weaseled out of the jam and went unscathed until Philadelphia's Howie Bedell touched him for a sacrifice fly. It was the third and last RBI of Bedell's career.

# LUCKY BREAK(DOWN)

In 1956, one John Morrissey was passing through Cooperstown merely to have his car repaired en route to a golf date. The *Life* magazine advertising executive decided to visit the Hall of Fame while he waited. To his astonishment, he was greeted as the Museum's 1,000,000th visitor and showered with a package of gifts that included season tickets to all major-league games, a lifetime pass to the Hall of Fame, an assortment of baseball literature, and a replica of a Bobby Thomson bat.

# WHEN BAD THINGS HAPPEN TO GOOD PLAYERS . . .

In a 1977 game, Catfish Hunter served up four home runs in a single inning.

In the 1934 World Series, Dizzy Dean ▶ was a baserunner when he threw himself in front of a potential double-play relay and was knocked unconscious.

John McGraw lost more World Series (six) than any manager in history.

Lou Brock led NL outfielders in errors seven times.

# RUBE FOSTER

Often hailed as "The Father of Black Baseball," Foster was a giant in every facet of the game.

**AS A PITCHER:** Won 44 straight games for the 1902 Cuban Giants...Went 51–5 for the 1905 White's Athletics.

**AS AN OWNER:** Created the Chicago American Giants, one of the most successful black teams ever...Won or shared three titles from 1914 to 1917.

**AS A MANAGER:** Managed for 20 years...Skippered the 1907 Leland Giants to a 110–10 record.

**AS A PIONEER:** Founded and was president of the Negro National League, the first successful Negro circuit.

"We are the ship, all else the sea."

—Inscription on the Negro National League letterhead

# HENRY CHADWICK

**PIONEER**  **ELECTED 1938**

- **Wrote** *The Game of Base Ball,* the first hardcover book on the game, 1868

- Credited with creating the modern box score, as well as developing the batting average and ERA statistics.

- Used his journalistic clout to get the infield fly rule adopted and eliminate ties by playing extra innings.

- Only journalist to be memorialized in the Hall of Fame itself instead of in the "writer's wing."

# MEMBERS OF THE
# BASEBALL HALL OF FAME

Percent of vote based on ballots from members of the Baseball Writers Association of America.
Lou Gehrig was inducted into the Hall of Fame under special circumstances.
Pioneer = off-the-field impact † = elected by Veterans Committee ‡ = elected from the Negro Leagues

| Year | Name | Position | Primary Career | Percent of vote |
|------|------|----------|----------------|-----------------|
| **1936** | Ty Cobb | CF | 1905–1928 | 98.23% |
| | Walter Johnson | P | 1907–1927 | 83.63% |
| | Christy Mathewson | P | 1900–1916 | 90.71% |
| | Babe Ruth | RF/P | 1914–1935 | 95.13% |
| | Honus Wagner | SS | 1897–1917 | 95.13% |
| **1937** | Morgan Bulkeley | Executive | | † |
| | Ban Johnson | Executive | | † |
| | Nap Lajoie | 2B | 1896–1916 | 83.58% |
| | Connie Mack | Mgr | 1894–1950 | † |
| | John McGraw | Mgr/3B | 1899, 1901–1932 | † |
| | Tris Speaker | CF | 1907–1928 | 82.09% |
| | George Wright | Pioneer | | † |
| | Cy Young | P | 1890–1911 | 76.12% |
| **1938** | Grover C. Alexander | P | 1911–1929 | 80.92% |
| | Alexander Cartwright | Pioneer | | † |
| | Henry Chadwick | Pioneer | | † |
| **1939** | Cap Anson | 1B | 1871–1897 | † |
| | Eddie Collins | 2B | 1906–1930 | 77.74% |

| Year | Name | Position | Primary Career | Percent of vote |
|------|------|----------|----------------|-----------------|
| **1939** | Charles Comiskey | Mgr/Executive | | † |
| | Candy Cummings | Pioneer | | † |
| | Buck Ewing | C | 1880–1897 | † |
| | Lou Gehrig | 1B | 1923–1939 | † |
| | Willie Keeler | RF | 1892–1910 | 75.55% |
| | Charles Radbourn | P | 1881–1891 | † |
| | George Sisler | 1B | 1915–1922, 1928 | 85.77% |
| | Albert Spalding | P/Executive | | † |
| **1940** | No elections | | | |
| **1941** | No elections | | | |
| **1942** | Rogers Hornsby | 2B | 1915–1937 | 78.11% |
| **1943** | No election | | | |
| **1944** | Kenesaw Mountain Landis | Executive | | † |
| **1945** | Roger Bresnahan | C | 1897, 1900–1915 | † |
| | Dan Brouthers | 1B | 1879–1896, 1904 | † |
| | Fred Clarke | LF/Mgr | 1894–1915 | † |
| | Jimmy Collins | 3B | 1895–1908 | † |
| | Ed Delahanty | LF | 1888–1903 | † |
| | Hugh Duffy | CF | 1888–1906 | † |
| | Hughie Jennings | SS/Mgr | 1891–1918 | † |
| | King Kelly | RF/C | 1878–1893 | † |
| | Jim O'Rourke | LF | 1872–1904 | † |
| | Wilbert Robinson | C/Mgr | 1902, 1914–1931 | † |

| Year | Name | Position | Primary Career | Percent of vote |
|---|---|---|---|---|
| 1946 | Jesse Burkett | LF | 1890–1905 | † |
| | Frank Chance | 1B/Mgr | 1898–1914 | † |
| | Jack Chesbro | P | 1899–1909 | † |
| | Johnny Evers | 2B | 1902–1917, 1922 | † |
| | Clark Griffith | P/Executive | | † |
| | Tommy McCarthy | RF | 1884–1896 | † |
| | Joe McGinnity | P | 1899–1908 | † |
| | Eddie Plank | P | 1901–1917 | † |
| | Joe Tinker | SS | 1902–1916 | † |
| | Rube Waddell | P | 1897, 1899–1910 | † |
| | Ed Walsh | P | 1904–1917 | † |
| 1947 | Mickey Cochrane | C | 1925–1937 | 79.5% |
| | Frankie Frisch | 2B | 1919–1937 | 84.47% |
| | Lefty Grove | P | 1925–1941 | 76.4% |
| | Carl Hubbell | P | 1928–1943 | 86.96% |
| 1948 | Herb Pennock | P | 1912–1934 | 77.69% |
| | Pie Traynor | 3B | 1920–1935, 1937 | 76.86% |
| 1949 | Mordecai Brown | P | 1903–1916 | † |
| | Charlie Gehringer | 2B | 1924–1942 | 85.03% |
| | Kid Nichols | P | 1890–1901, 1904–1906 | † |
| 1950 | None elected | | | |
| 1951 | Jimmie Foxx | 1B | 1925–1942, 1944–1945 | 79.2% |
| | Mel Ott | RF | 1926–1947 | 87.17% |

| Year | Name | Position | Primary Career | Percent of vote |
|------|------|----------|----------------|-----------------|
| 1952 | Harry Heilmann | RF | 1914, 1916–1931 | 86.75% |
|  | Paul Waner | RF | 1926–1940 | 83.33% |
| 1953 | Ed Barrow | Executive |  | † |
|  | Chief Bender | P | 1903–1917, 1925 | † |
|  | Tommy Connolly | Umpire |  | † |
|  | Dizzy Dean | P | 1930, 1932–1941, 1947 | 79.17% |
|  | Bill Klem | Umpire |  | † |
|  | Al Simmons | LF | 1924–1941, 1943–1944 | 75.38% |
|  | Bobby Wallace | SS | 1894–1918 | † |
|  | Harry Wright | Mgr/Pioneer |  | † |
| 1954 | Bill Dickey | C | 1928–1943, 1946 | 80.16% |
|  | Rabbit Maranville | SS | 1912–1933, 1935 | 82.94% |
|  | Bill Terry | 1B | 1923–1936 | 77.38% |
| 1955 | Frank Baker | 3B | 1908–1914, 1916–1919, 1921–1922 | † |
|  | Joe DiMaggio | CF | 1936–1942, 1946–1951 | 88.84% |
|  | Gabby Hartnett | C | 1922–1941 | 77.69% |
|  | Ted Lyons | P | 1923–1942, 1946 | 86.45% |
|  | Ray Schalk | C | 1912–1929 | † |
|  | Dazzy Vance | P | 1915, 1918, 1922–1935 | 81.67% |
| 1956 | Joe Cronin | SS | 1926–1945 | 78.76% |
|  | Hank Greenberg | 1B | 1930, 1933–1941, 1945–1947 | 84.97% |
| 1957 | Sam Crawford | RF | 1899–1917 | † |
|  | Joe McCarthy | Mgr | 1926–1946, 1948–1950 | † |

| Year | Name | Position | Primary Career | Percent of vote |
|------|------|----------|----------------|-----------------|
| 1958 | None elected | | | |
| 1959 | Zack Wheat | LF | 1909–1927 | † |
| 1960 | None elected | | | |
| 1961 | Max Carey | CF | 1910–1929 | † |
| | Billy Hamilton | CF | 1888–1901 | † |
| 1962 | Bob Feller | P | 1936–1941, 1945–1956 | 93.75% |
| | Bill McKechnie | Mgr | 1915, 1922–1926, 1928–1946 | † |
| | Jackie Robinson | 2B | 1945, 1947–1956 | 77.5% |
| | Edd Roush | CF | 1913–1929, 1931 | † |
| 1963 | John Clarkson | P | 1882, 1884–1894 | † |
| | Elmer Flick | RF | 1898–1910 | † |
| | Sam Rice | RF | 1915–1934 | † |
| | Eppa Rixey | P | 1912–1917, 1919–1933 | † |
| 1964 | Luke Appling | SS | 1930–1943, 1945–1950 | 84% |
| | Red Faber | P | 1914–1933 | † |
| | Burleigh Grimes | P | 1916–1934 | † |
| | Miller Huggins | 2B/Mgr | 1913–1929 | † |
| | Tim Keefe | P | 1880–1893 | † |
| | Heinie Manush | LF | 1923–1939 | † |
| | Monte Ward | P/SS | 1878–1894 | † |
| 1965 | Pud Galvin | P | 1875, 1879–1892 | † |
| 1966 | Casey Stengel | Mgr | 1934–1936, 1938–1943, 1946–1960, 1962–1965 | † |

| Year | Name | Position | Primary Career | Percent of vote |
|------|------|----------|----------------|-----------------|
| 1966 | Ted Williams | LF | 1939–1942, 1946–1960 | 93.38% |
| 1967 | Branch Rickey | Executive | | † |
| | Red Ruffing | P | 1924–1942, 1945–1947 | 86.93% |
| | Lloyd Waner | CF | 1927–1942, 1944–1945 | † |
| 1968 | Kiki Cuyler | RF | 1921–1938 | † |
| | Goose Goslin | LF | 1921–1938 | † |
| | Joe Medwick | LF | 1932–1948 | 84.81% |
| 1969 | Roy Campanella | C | 1948–1957 | 79.41% |
| | Stan Coveleski | P | 1912, 1916–1928 | † |
| | Waite Hoyt | P | 1918–1938 | † |
| | Stan Musial | LF/1B | 1941–1944, 1946–1963 | 93.24% |
| 1970 | Lou Boudreau | SS | 1938–1952 | 77.33% |
| | Earle Combs | CF | 1924–1935 | † |
| | Ford Frick | Executive | | † |
| | Jesse Haines | P | 1918, 1920–1937 | † |
| 1971 | Dave Bancroft | SS | 1915–1930 | † |
| | Jake Beckley | 1B | 1888–1907 | † |
| | Chick Hafey | LF | 1924–1935, 1937 | † |
| | Harry Hooper | RF | 1909–1925 | † |
| | Joe Kelley | LF | 1891–1906, 1908 | † |
| | Rube Marquard | P | 1908–1925 | † |
| | Satchel Paige | P | 1927–1953, 1955, 1965 | ‡ |
| | George Weiss | Executive | | † |

| Year | Name | Position | Primary Career | Percent of vote |
|------|------|----------|----------------|-----------------|
| 1972 | Yogi Berra | C | 1946–1963, 1965 | 85.61% |
| | Josh Gibson | C | 1930–1946 | ‡ |
| | Lefty Gomez | P | 1930–1943 | † |
| | Will Harridge | Executive | 1909–1925 | † |
| | Sandy Koufax | P | 1955–1966 | 86.87% |
| | Buck Leonard | 1B | 1933–1950 | ‡ |
| | Early Wynn | P | 1939–1945, 1946–1962 | 76.01% |
| | Ross Youngs | RF | 1917–1926 | † |
| 1973 | Roberto Clemente | RF | 1955–1972 | 92.69% |
| | Billy Evans | Umpire | | † |
| | Monte Irvin | LF | 1937–1942, 1945–1956 | ‡ |
| | George Kelly | 1B | 1915–1917, 1919–1930, 1932 | † |
| | Warren Spahn | P | 1942, 1946–1965 | 82.89% |
| | Mickey Welch | P | 1880–1892 | † |
| 1974 | Cool Papa Bell | CF | 1922–1938, 1942, 1947–1950 | ‡ |
| | Jim Bottomley | 1B | 1922–1937 | † |
| | Jocko Conlan | Umpire | 1942, 1946–1965 | 82.89% |
| | Whitey Ford | P | 1950, 1953–1967 | 77.81% |
| | Mickey Mantle | CF | 1951–1968 | 88.22% |
| | Sam Thompson | RF | 1885–1898, 1908 | † |
| 1975 | Earl Averill | CF | 1930–1941 | † |
| | Bucky Harris | Mgr | 1924–1943, 1947–1948, 1950–1956 | † |
| | Billy Herman | 2B | 1931–1943, 1946–1947 | † |

| Year | Name | Position | Primary Career | Percent of vote |
|------|------|----------|----------------|-----------------|
| 1975 | Judy Johnson | 3B | 1918–1937 | ‡ |
|  | Ralph Kiner | LF | 1946–1955 | 75.41% |
| 1976 | Oscar Charleston | CF | 1915–1950, 1954 | ‡ |
|  | Roger Connor | 1B | 1880–1897 | † |
|  | Cal Hubbard | Umpire |  | † |
|  | Bob Lemon | P | 1946–1958 | 78.61% |
|  | Freddy Lindstrom | 3B | 1924–1935 | 75.41% |
|  | Robin Roberts | P | 1948–1966 | 86.86% |
| 1977 | Ernie Banks | SS/1B | 1953–1971 | 83.81% |
|  | Martín Dihigo | P/2B | 1923–1931, 1935–1936, 1945 | ‡ |
|  | John Henry "Pop" Lloyd | SS | 1906–1932 | ‡ |
|  | Al Lopez | C/Mgr | 1951–1965, 1968–1969 | † |
|  | Amos Rusie | P | 1889–1895, 1897–1898, 1901 | † |
|  | Joe Sewell | SS | 1920–1933 | † |
| 1978 | Addie Joss | P | 1902–1910 | † |
|  | Larry MacPhail | Executive |  | † |
|  | Eddie Mathews | 3B | 1952–1968 | 79.42% |
| 1979 | Warren Giles | Executive |  | † |
|  | Willie Mays | CF | 1948–1973 | 94.68% |
|  | Hack Wilson | CF | 1923–1934 | † |
| 1980 | Al Kaline | RF | 1953–1974 | 88.31% |
|  | Chuck Klein | CF | 1928–1944 | † |
|  | Duke Snider | CF | 1947–1964 | 86.49% |

| Year | Name | Position | Primary Career | Percent of vote |
|------|------|----------|----------------|-----------------|
| 1980 | Tom Yawkey | Executive | | † |
| 1981 | Rube Foster | P/Mgr | 1902–1926 | † |
| | Bob Gibson | P | 1959–1975 | 84.04% |
| | Johnny Mize | 1B | 1936–1942, 1946–1953 | † |
| 1982 | Hank Aaron | RF | 1952, 1954–1976 | 97.83% |
| | Albert "Happy" Chandler | Executive | | † |
| | Travis Jackson | SS | 1922–1936 | † |
| | Frank Robinson | RF | 1956–1976 | 89.16% |
| 1983 | Walter Alston | Mgr | 1954–1976 | † |
| | George Kell | 3B | 1943–1957 | † |
| | Juan Marichal | P | 1960–1975 | 83.69% |
| | Brooks Robinson | 3B | 1955–1977 | 91.98% |
| 1984 | Luis Aparicio | SS | 1956–1973 | 84.62% |
| | Don Drysdale | P | 1956–1969 | 78.41% |
| | Rick Ferrell | C | 1929–1945, 1947 | † |
| | Harmon Killebrew | 1B/3B | 1954–1975 | 83.13% |
| | Pee Wee Reese | SS | 1940–1942, 1946–1958 | † |
| 1985 | Lou Brock | LF | 1961–1979 | 79.75% |
| | Enos Slaughter | RF | 1938–1959 | † |
| | Arky Vaughan | SS | 1932–1943, 1947–1948 | † |
| | Hoyt Wilhelm | P | 1952–1972 | 83.8% |
| 1986 | Bobby Doerr | 2B | 1937–1944, 1946–1951 | † |
| | Ernie Lombardi | C | 1931–1947 | † |

| Year | Name | Position | Primary Career | Percent of vote |
|---|---|---|---|---|
| 1986 | Willie McCovey | 1B | 1959–1980 | 81.41% |
| 1987 | Ray Dandridge | 3B | 1933–1939, 1942, 1944, 1949 | † |
| | Catfish Hunter | P | 1965–1979 | 76.27% |
| | Billy Williams | LF | 1959–1976 | 85.71% |
| 1988 | Willie Stargell | LF | 1962–1982 | 82.44% |
| 1989 | Al Barlick | Umpire | | † |
| | Johnny Bench | C | 1967–1983 | 96.42% |
| | Red Schoendienst | 2B | 1945–1963 | † |
| | Carl Yastrzemski | LF/1B | 1961–1983 | 94.63% |
| 1990 | Joe Morgan | 2B | 1963–1984 | 81.76% |
| | Jim Palmer | P | 1965–1984 | 92.57% |
| 1991 | Rod Carew | 2B/1B | 1967–1985 | 90.52% |
| | Ferguson Jenkins | P | 1965–1983 | 75.4% |
| | Tony Lazzeri | 2B | 1926–1939 | † |
| | Gaylord Perry | P | 1962–1983 | 77.2% |
| | Bill Veeck | Executive | | † |
| 1992 | Rollie Fingers | P | 1968–1982, 1984–1985 | 81.16% |
| | Bill McGowan | Umpire | | † |
| | Hal Newhouser | P | 1939–1955 | † |
| | Tom Seaver | P | 1967–1986 | 98.84% |
| 1993 | Reggie Jackson | RF | 1967–1987 | 93.62% |
| 1994 | Steve Carlton | P | 1965–1988 | 95.82% |
| | Leo Durocher | Mgr | 1939–1946, 1948–1955, 1966–1973 | † |

| Year | Name | Position | Primary Career | Percent of vote |
|------|------|----------|----------------|-----------------|
| 1994 | Phil Rizzuto | SS | 1941–1942, 1946–1956 | † |
| 1995 | Richie Ashburn | CF | 1948–1962 | † |
| | Leon Day | P | 1934–1939, 1941–1943, 1946, 1949–1950 | † |
| | William Hulbert | Executive | | † |
| | Mike Schmidt | 3B | 1972–1989 | 96.52% |
| | Vic Willis | P | 1898–1910 | † |
| 1996 | Jim Bunning | P | 1955–1971 | † |
| | Bill Foster | P | 1923–1938 | † |
| | Ned Hanlon | Mgr | 1889–1890, 1892–1907 | † |
| | Earl Weaver | Mgr | 1968–1982, 1985–1986 | † |
| 1997 | Nellie Fox | 2B | 1947–1965 | † |
| | Tommy Lasorda | Mgr | 1976–1996 | † |
| | Phil Niekro | P | 1964–1987 | 80.34% |
| | Willie Wells | SS | 1923, 1924–1936, 1942, 1944–1948 | † |
| 1998 | George Davis | SS | 1890–1909 | † |
| | Larry Doby | CF | 1942–1943, 1946–1959 | † |
| | Lee MacPhail | Executive | | † |
| | Bullet Rogan | P | 1917, 1920–1938 | † |
| | Don Sutton | P | 1966–1988 | 81.6% |
| 1999 | George Brett | 3B | 1973–1993 | 98.19% |
| | Orlando Cepeda | 1B | 1958–1974 | † |
| | Nestor Chylak | Umpire | | † |

| Year | Name | Position | Primary Career | Percent of vote |
|---|---|---|---|---|
| 1999 | Nolan Ryan | P | 1966, 1968–1993 | 98.79% |
| | Frank Selee | Mgr | 1890, 1892–1905 | † |
| | Smokey Joe Williams | P | 1910–1932 | † |
| | Robin Yount | SS/CF | 1974–1993 | 77.46% |
| 2000 | Sparky Anderson | Mgr | 1970–1995 | † |
| | Carlton Fisk | C | 1969, 1971–1993 | 79.56% |
| | Bid McPhee | 2B | 1882–1899 | † |
| | Tony Perez | 1B | 1964–1986 | 77.15% |
| | Turkey Stearnes | CF | 1920–1942, 1945 | † |
| 2001 | Bill Mazeroski | 2B | 1956–1972 | † |
| | Kirby Puckett | CF | 1984–1995 | 82.14% |
| | Hilton Smith | P | 1932–1948 | † |
| | Dave Winfield | RF | 1973–1988, 1990–1995 | 84.47% |
| 2002 | Ozzie Smith | SS | 1978–1996 | 91.74% |
| 2003 | Gary Carter | C | 1974–1992 | 78.02% |
| | Eddie Murray | 1B | 1977–1997 | 85.28% |
| 2004 | Dennis Eckersley | P | 1975–1998 | 83.2% |
| | Paul Molitor | DH/3B | 1978–1998 | 85.2% |
| 2005 | Wade Boggs | 3B | 1982–1999 | 91.86% |
| | Ryne Sandberg | 2B | 1981–1994, 1996–1997 | 76.16% |
| 2006 | Ray Brown | P | 1931–1945 | ‡ |
| | Willard Brown | RF | 1935–1950 | ‡ |
| | Andy Cooper | P | 1920–1941 | ‡ |

| Year | Name | Position | Primary Career | Percent of vote |
|------|------|----------|----------------|-----------------|
| 2006 | Frank Grant | 2B | 1886–1903 | ‡ |
| | Pete Hill | LF | 1899–1926 | ‡ |
| | Biz Mackey | C | 1920–1947 | ‡ |
| | Effa Manley | Executive | | ‡ |
| | José Méndez | P | 1908–1926 | ‡ |
| | Alex Pompez | Executive | | ‡ |
| | Cumberland Posey | Executive | | ‡ |
| | Louis Santop | C | 1909–1926 | ‡ |
| | Bruce Sutter | P | 1976–1988 | 76.9% |
| | Mule Suttles | 1B/LF | 1921, 1923–1944 | ‡ |
| | Ben Taylor | 1B | 1908–1929 | ‡ |
| | Cristóbal Torriente | CF | 1913–1928 | ‡ |
| | Sol White | Pioneer | | ‡ |
| | J. L. Wilkinson | Executive | | ‡ |
| | Jud Wilson | 3B/1B | 1922–1945 | ‡ |
| 2007 | Cal Ripken, Jr. | SS | 1981–2001 | 98.5% |
| | Tony Gwynn | RF | 1982–2001 | 97.6% |
| 2008 | Barney Dreyfuss | Executive | | † |
| | Goose Gossage | P | 1972–1989, 1991–1994 | 85.8% |
| | Bowie Kuhn | Executive | | † |
| | Walter O'Malley | Executive | | † |
| | Billy Southworth | Mgr | 1929, 1940–1951 | † |
| | Dick Williams | Mgr | 1967–1969, 1971–1988 | † |

# INDEX

# Acknowledgments

Page 14: Reprinted with permission from *Baseball Digest.*

Page 64: From the book *This Is Not a Novel* by David Markson. Copyright © 2001. Published by Counterpoint Press. Used by Permission.

Page 66: Reprinted by agreement with the Estate of Martin Luther King, Jr., c/o Writers House as agent for the proprietor, New York, N.Y. Copyright © Martin Luther King, Jr., Copyright © renewed Coretta Scott King.

Page 67: Reprinted with permission from *Baseball Digest.*

Page 78: An excerpt from the obituary "Pee Wee Was a Giant" written by Jon Thurber and Jason Reid, published August 15, 1999. Copyright © 1999. Reprinted with permission from *Los Angeles Times.*

Page 227: Reprinted from *Maybe I'll Pitch Forever* by Leroy (Satchel) Paige by permission of the University of Nebraska Press.

# Photo Credits

**Front cover:**
**Getty Images** MLB Photos (top right); **PIL Collection** (top left, bottom left & bottom right).

**Back cover:**
**Transcendental Graphics** Mark Rucker

**AP Wide World Photos:** 64–65; **AU Sports Memorabilia:** 95 (center); **Compliments of the Candy Wrapper Museum:** 142 (right); **Getty Images:** 4, 6, 8, 26, 27, 43, 48, 50, 60, 61, 80, 81, 98 (bottom), 108, 109, 118–119, 121, 128, 136, 171, 180 (left), 240, 245 (bottom left), 246, 248–249, 259, 264, 274, 275, 276, 290, 291, 292, 297; Diamond Images, 17, 20, 56, 76–77, 186–187, 214, 220, 243; Focus On Sports, 38, 143, 157, 163, 165, 169, 177, 208–209, 228, 232, 247, 257, 285; MLB Photos, 14 (left), 59, 68, 70 (top), 85, 89, 91, 93, 98 (top), 110, 115 (right center), 120, 125, 152, 164, 172, 180 (right), 181 (right), 192, 201, 217, 230, 244, 245 (top center & bottom left), 250, 256, 273, 279; **Index Stock Imagery, Inc.:** Omni Photo Communications Inc., 33; Barry Winiker, 5; **iStockphoto:** 44–45; **National Baseball Hall of Fame Library, Cooperstown, N.Y.:** 12–13, 25, 49, 52 (center & bottom), 57, 62, 70 (bottom), 71, 73, 86, 94 (top center, center & bottom), 95 (top right), 97, 104, 105, 111, 113, 115 (top left & top right), 122, 123, 126, 127, 129, 131, 132, 144, 149, 154, 156, 158, 168, 173, 175, 176, 178, 181 (left), 183 (top right), 193 (top right), 194, 195, 203, 207, 212, 213, 219, 224, 225, 229, 231, 233, 234, 238, 251, 252, 253, 254, 255 (bottom), 258, 260, 261, 265, 266, 267, 268 (top left & top right), 271, 280, 282, 283, 288, 289, 294 (left center), 298, 299; **PhotoDisc Collection:** 18–19, 29, 39, 41, 55, 63, 87, 116, 185, 222, 223; **PIL Collection:** 11, 14 (right), 15, 16, 23, 24 (top & bottom), 34, 35, 36, 37, 42, 46, 47, 51, 52 (top left, left center & right center), 53 (left center, right center & bottom), 54, 67, 69, 75, 78, 79, 82, 83, 84, 88, 90, 92, 94 (top left & top right), 95 (top), 96, 99, 101, 103, 106, 112, 115 (left center), 117, 124, 133, 137, 138, 139, 140, 141, 146, 147, 150, 151, 153, 159, 160, 161, 162, 167, 170, 174, 179, 182, 183 (top left, right center, left center & bottom right), 184, 188, 189, 190, 191, 193 (top left & right center), 196, 197, 199, 202, 204, 205, 206, 210, 211, 215, 216, 218, 226, 227, 235, 236, 239, 241, 245 (top left, top right, far left center, left center, right center, far right center & bottom left center), 255 (top), 262 (top & bottom), 268 (center, right center & bottom left), 269, 270, 272, 281, 286, 287, 293, 294 (top left, top right & bottom right), 295; **SuperStock:** 114, 142 (center), 148, 200, 237; Michael P. Gadomski, 31, 296; Susan Goines, 28, 263; David Spindel, 21, 24 (center), 58, 74, 102, 130, 145, 166, 221, 262, 278, 295; Medford Taylor, 32; **Transcendental Graphics:** Charles Conlan, 53 (top), 155, 193 (left center); Mark Rucker, 22, 40, 52 (top right), 72, 100, 115 (bottom left), 134, 135, 193 (bottom).

DONALD SCOTT DRYSDALE
BROOKLYN N.L. 1956-1957
LOS ANGELES N.L. 1958-1969

ROBERTO WALKER CLEMENTE
PITTSBURGH N.L. 1955-1972

HENRY "HANK" AARON
MILWAUKEE N.L. 1954-1965
ATLANTA N.L. 1966-1974

BROOKS CALBERT ROBINSON, JR.
BALTIMORE A.L. 1955-1977

LUIS ERNESTO APARICIO
CHICAGO A.L. 1956-1962, 1968-1970
BALTIMORE A.L. 1963-1967
BOSTON A.L. 1971-1973

WILLIE LEE McCOVEY
PIRATES

JUAN ANTONIO
(SANCHEZ) MARICHAL
SAN FRANCISCO N.L. 1960-1973

ROBERT GIBSON
ST. LOUIS N.L. 1959-1975

JAMES PAUL DAVID BUNNING

EDWIN LEE MATHEWS
BOSTON N.L. MILWAUKEE N.L.
ATLANTA N.L. HOUSTON N.L.
DETROIT A.L. 1952-1968

WILVER DORNEL STARGELL
"POPS"
PITTSBURGH N.L. 1962-1982

EARL SIDNEY WEAVER
BALTIMORE A.L. 1968-1982, 1985-1986

LOUIS CLARK BROCK
CHICAGO N.L. 1961-1964
ST. LOUIS N.L. 1964-1979

LEO ERNEST DUROCHER
"THE LIP"

FRANK FRISCH